AF893945

SPINELESS

To Mike Hurrell and Sue Boyd

SPINELESS

Dealing with pests and pals in your home and backyard

BRONWEN SCOTT

JACANA BOOKS

ALLEN & UNWIN

The pages of this book are printed on paper derived from forests promoting sustainable forest management. For more info go to: www.pefc.org

First published in 2009

Copyright © Bronwen Scott 2009

All rights reserved. No part of this book may be reproduced or transmitted in any form or by any means, electronic or mechanical, including photocopying, recording or by any information storage and retrieval system, without prior permission in writing from the publisher. The Australian *Copyright Act 1968* (the Act) allows a maximum of one chapter or 10 per cent of this book, whichever is the greater, to be photocopied by any educational institution for its educational purposes provided that the educational institution (or body that administers it) has given a remuneration notice to Copyright Agency Limited (CAL) under the Act.

Jacana Books, an imprint of
Allen & Unwin
83 Alexander Street
Crows Nest NSW 2065
Australia
Phone: (61 2) 8425 0100
Fax: (61 2) 9906 2218
Email: info@allenandunwin.com
Web: www.allenandunwin.com

Cataloguing-in-publication details are available
from the National Library of Australia
www.librariesaustralia.nla.gov.au

ISBN 978 1 74175 836 8

Internal design by Nada Backovic
Internal photographs MBPhoto/iStockphoto and Arlindo/iStockphoto
Set in 12/16 pt Adobe Garamond by Midland Typesetters, Australia
Printed in Australia by McPherson's Printing Group

10 9 8 7 6 5 4 3 2 1

CONTENTS

INTRODUCTION

The Spineless are everywhere.

We share our lives with them. Oh, we might think we're in charge, but they're the ones that drive the world. A bit far-fetched, you say? Not at all. What would happen if they disappeared?

Picture this. All the flies have vanished. Gone. It doesn't matter where. They could have fallen victim to some fly-specific plague or been abducted by aliens. Details aren't important. But (for whatever reason) the flies, like Elvis, have left the building.

A world free of flies might sound like an attractive proposition. Really, what's the worst that could happen? A barbecue without the great Australian salute. A decline in plastic wrap sales. Right? Right. For a while. But it wouldn't take long before their absence had other consequences. The sort of consequences you might not want to think about too deeply. But let's do that, anyway.

Dead animals—why aren't we knee-deep in them? Given the number that must drop off the twig each day, they should be piling up around the place in rotting drifts. Yet they aren't.

We can thank all the blowflies and flesh flies, among others, for their free waste-removal service. When something dies, they arrive within minutes to lay their eggs on the carcass. On hatching, the baby flies (maggots) make short work of the remains. What's disgusting to us is delicious to them. And that's a good thing because without their decay-loving palates, we'd be wading through dunes of decomposing mice and pigeons. And that's not all they feed on, by the way. Just don't make me talk about the other items on a maggot's lunch menu. The items that were on your lunch menu only the day before.

So that's one thing that the Spineless do to make the world run smoothly. A pretty important thing, you'd have to concede. But do they do anything else? Ha! Does a bear leave food for flies in the woods?

The Spineless pollinate plants. Without bees, wasps, beetles, bugs, butterflies, moths and flies we'd lose a load of fruit and vegetables, flowers and trees.

They also break down leaves and enrich soil. Under every rock and log and in the heart of every compost heap, the Spineless turn trash into fertiliser.

They are food for other animals. After all, where would bee-eaters be without bees?

And there's more, of course, both good and bad. Without the Spineless the world would be a very different place.

Now, I know what you're thinking. That's all fine but they've got the whole planet to buzz around in so why have they moved into my garden? Why have they settled in my house? To answer that, try thinking like a beetle. (Or a snail or millipede . . . Take your pick.) What's the world like when you're only a centimetre long? At that scale, you can't distinguish between a lawn and a patch of grassland or a hedge and a forest. So where the human sees a laundry cupboard, a spider sees the dark corner of a cave, an ideal place to set a web to catch dinner.

WHAT ARE THE SPINELESS?

(We can sing this.) They're just about everything, man, just about everything. (Take a deep breath.) They're flatworms, jellyfish, coral, earthworms, leeches, garden snails, fleas and butterflies, moths and beetles, crabs and crayfish, sea stars . . . You get the idea. They're a wild bunch of odd-looking critters with anywhere between zero and two pairs of wings, zero and four pairs of eyes, and zero and a hundred or more pairs of legs. They live in the sea, in fresh water and on land. Some of them even live inside other animals. (The Alien was an amateur!) Between them, the Spineless have the whole world covered.

Although the members of this strange bunch don't always have a family resemblance, they are grouped together by one feature—they all lack a backbone. I don't mean metaphorically as in they're short on courage. I mean literally as in they're short on bones. Back bones, in particular, but any sort in general. Even the critters that go crunch underfoot are entirely free of them. (The crunch comes from shells and other parts. As we'll hear more about soon.) The term given by biologists to the whole group is 'invertebrates'. Translated from Latin it means 'lacking vertebrae', which are the small bones that make up a spine.

But if they don't have backbones, how do the Spineless move around on land?

The short answer is—they do it very well. There's more than a million species of insects and almost all of them live on land. They don't seem to experience any difficulty in getting about, even in flying.

But insects are only some of the members of this motley bunch. Because the Spineless are such a mixed bag, they move in different ways.

Squishy animals like worms and slugs don't have legs. Instead, they shift by contracting their muscles and shunting around fluid within their bodies. It's not a technique that permits zippy progress so animals that move in this way either feed on other slowcoaches or on things that stay in one place. There are a few exceptions, of course. There usually are. Among them are the velvet worms (p. 39), which have multiple hydraulically operated legs that can carry them along at a cracking pace. What prey they can't run down, they immobilise by shooting out glue from glands on their heads. (Beat *that*, Spiderman!)

Other squishies get around by laying down a carpet of mucus and sliding over it on a fringe of microscopic hairs (cilia). Not elegant but definitely effective. Those shiny trails on the concrete? They're the leftovers from a slug's or snail's nocturnal wanderings.

Crunchy animals, such as insects, slaters and scorpions, have six or more legs, so they can crawl, scuttle or hop to their heart's content. (Yes, they do have hearts.) They lack an internal skeleton—no bones, remember—so all the hard stuff is on the outside. These critters are covered in a casing that is thick and rigid in some spots and soft and flexible in others. The result is a one-piece suit of armour that both protects and supports. Muscles run directly from the inner surface of one plate to the next in a system of winches and levers. This combination of components lets them move rapidly. It also gives them the ability to fly. And in the same way that an internal skeleton has allowed backboned animals to diversify into the amazing range of fish, amphibians, reptiles, birds and mammals (including us), the external skeleton (exoskeleton) has given rise to an even more extraordinary assortment of invertebrates.

Okay. We know there's over a million different types of insects. So just how many Spineless are there?

Insects make up by far the biggest proportion (although recent research suggests the nematode worms are giving them a run for their money). Biologists have put scientific names to almost 1,250,000 species, but there are millions more yet to be described. A lot of those are sitting in museum collections waiting for scientists to study them. Some of those unnamed species may even live in your garden.

From what we know of biodiversity, the Spineless make up more than 95 per cent of species in the animal kingdom. But that's not all. Not only do invertebrates come in a huge variety, they're also here in great numbers. It's hardly surprising they've taken over your garden. When it comes to animals, this is truly a Spineless world.

HOW TO USE THIS BOOK

There's a critter in your house or garden and you want to find out something about it. What is it? What does it do? How do I encourage it to stay or persuade it to move on? So what's the quickest and easiest way of locating that information in this book?

That depends on your starting point. If you haven't seen the animal but have noticed souvenirs of its visit, such as nibbled leaves, burrows in the lawn or other mementos, the 'What's doing this?' guide on p. 10 will give you a lead to follow.

If you're looking at it from a distance (possibly from on top of a chair), the quickest way to identify your animal is to note its general shape and the way in which it moves. I've divided up this book by form and movement: long and thin; hoppers and skippers; eight-legged crawlers; six-legged crawlers; and fliers. (There are no entries for 'Aaargh! Moves like a rocket'. Perhaps in the next edition.) As well as these sections, there is also one on the common non-spineless animals that are pals and pests in the house and garden. I've included these because many play key roles in keeping the spineless under control. Finally, there's a section on the weird traces that the Spineless leave around the place.

If you've got the critter right in front of you, the pictures on p. 12—'What does it look like?'—will point you in the right direction.

You may not be able to identify your new companion precisely. Thousands of species of animals live in gardens across Australia. A backyard in Broome won't get the same range of visitors as a backyard in Hobart. And they'll both be different from the guest list in Alice Springs. But this book will help you narrow it down to a group. And if that doesn't satisfy your appetite for knowledge, there's a list of useful sources—books, museums and websites—at the end of this book that will keep you going.

Now, having got an idea of your visitor's identity, the next question to ask might be: is it a pal or pest?

Pals are defined here as those animals that either are helpful to us (because they eat pests) or don't do any damage. Pests are the obvious troublemakers—leaf-chompers, fruit-spoilers, stingers and biters. They're the ones that cause major problems.

But you know that this isn't always a neat division. We sometimes need to weigh up cost against benefit. A bucketload of animals can do pesky, pesty things but are also really useful. (Spiders, for example.) Do you boot 'em out or let them stay? Others might inflict a small amount of damage—in which case it boils down to a matter of personal preference. Do you want an immaculate garden or are you okay with the odd scratch and dent? This book puts them into broad categories. The finetuning is down to you.

So, you know what's in your garden and whether they're pals or pests (or both). The next step is working out how to evict the pests and welcome the pals. Under every entry, there's a short section that mentions the common methods used to do this. There's more detailed information on traps, baits and sprays in the chapter called 'Keeping pests under control' (p. 204).

And if an encounter between you and your house and garden visitors goes wrong, there's also a chapter on first aid (p. 220). Let's hope those pages remain unthumbed.

What's doing this?

Webs

Bites and itches

Holes in fabric

Curled leaves

Holes in paper

Holes in the lawn or mulch

Cicadas *p. 71*
Rabbits *p. 145*
Land crayfish *p. 202*
White-winged choughs *p. 161*
Bandicoots *p. 140*
Blackbirds *p. 153*
Crickets *p. 83*
Spiders *p. 48*
Cats *p. 148*

Bite marks in leaves or skeletonised leaves

Caterpillars *p. 26*
Cherry or pear slugs *p. 23*
Leaf-cutter bees *p. 117*
Spitfires *p. 24*

Lumps and bumps on leaves

Scale insects *p.198*
Galls *p. 201*

Scribbles on leaves

Leaf-mining insects *p. 195*

Noises: trills, chirps and buzzes

Frogs *p. 125*
Cicadas *p. 71*
Mole crickets *p. 83*
Flies, including mosquitoes *p. 104*
Birds (obviously) *p. 153*
Grasshoppers and katydids *p. 41*
Field crickets *p. 83*
Wasps *p. 119*
Bees *p. 116*

Scribbles on trees

Scribbly gum moth *p. 112*
Beetle larvae *p. 32*

What does it look like?

Long and thin? *pp. 14–40*

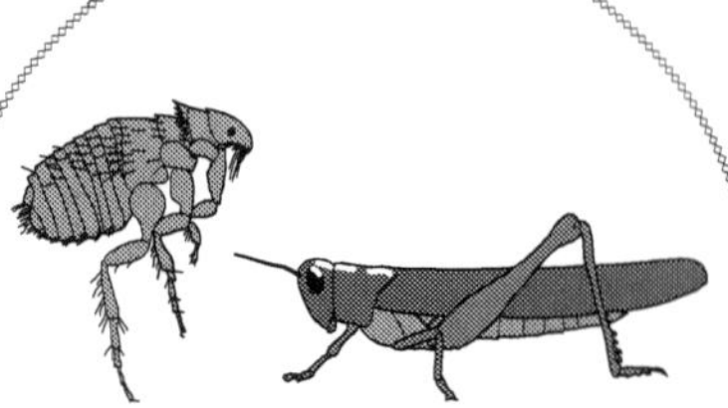

Hopping, skipping or jumping? *pp. 41–7*

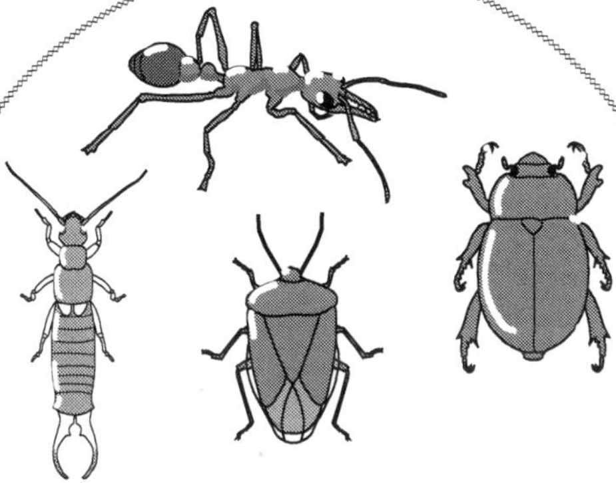

Six legs and crawling? *pp. 62–99*

Flying? *pp. 104–23*

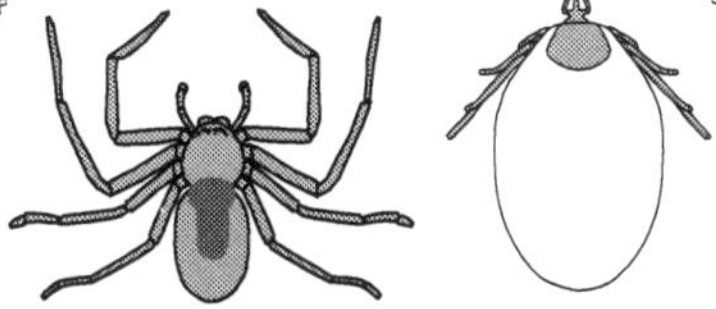

Eight legs and crawling? *pp. 48–61*

Snail or slug? *pp. 100–3*

LONG AND THIN: WRIGGLERS AND GRUBS

EARTHWORMS

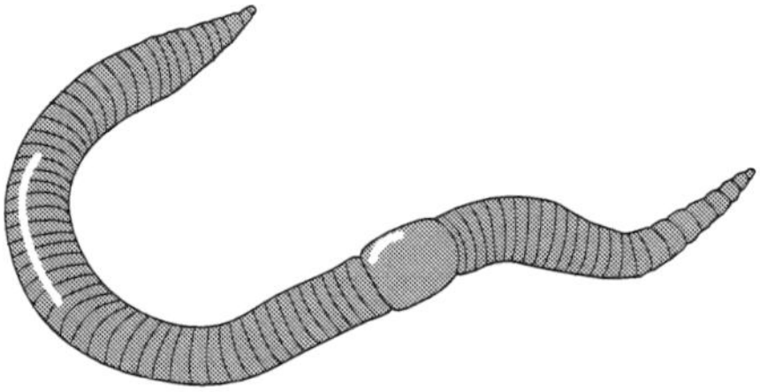

Short fat slimy ones, long thin skinny ones . . . The earthworm is the most frequently seen worm in the garden. It has a characteristic appearance—the slender pink, brown or grey body looks as though it is divided into rings. Adult earthworms have a wide 'collar' near the front end.

Earthworms move in a way that's all their own. First they stre-e-e-etch out and anchor themselves with tiny bristles, too small to see without a magnifying glass. Then they contract, bringing the tail end forward. The technique is used both for crawling across the ground and for burrowing through soil. No other common garden worm-type critter gets around in this style.

The name tells only part of their story. Earthworms spend most of their lives in soil and compost, emerging at night or on cool and rainy days. Some dig permanent burrows, whereas others wander through the dirt. Some live deep below the surface; the rest roam around the topsoil. You might find these roamers under logs, rocks and plant pots. Whichever type they are, *all* earthworms prefer to be where it is cool and damp and where there are plenty of dead leaves to eat.

Earthworms enrich soil by turning those leaves and other materials into humus. There's nothing fancy about the process. A hungry earthworm swallows dead leaves along with bits of soil, which its grinds up all together in a digestive mill called the gizzard. What emerges from the other end is worm poo loaded with nutrients. Some species of earthworms are so efficient at this conversion that they are farmed commercially and their poo sold as a liquid or solid fertiliser.

But that's not all that worms do. Their burrowing activity opens up channels that allow water and air to penetrate the soil and prevent compaction. Let's not mince words: earthworms are great for the garden.

Pal or pest?
Every gardener wants earthworms.

How do I deal with them?

You can encourage garden earthworms by giving them plenty to eat. Leaf mulch is an excellent start. It provides not only dinner but also the cool, moist conditions that they love. Laying off the pesticides is also a good idea. Earthworms don't take too kindly to them.

If you're *really* serious, you can set up your own backyard farm. Your ranched worms will apply their Midas touch by transforming kitchen scraps and garden waste into nutrient-rich compost.

Large wooden or foam containers (such as broccoli boxes from your local greengrocers) are best for a home farm. The simplest version is a box or bin, which can be emptied on the garden once the worms have done their stuff. Every wriggler-rancher has a favourite recipe but the key to healthy worms is moisture, good drainage and a decent supply of food. Avoid onions, citrus scraps, meat and dairy products. And *never* add anything containing poisonous chemicals.

Effective composters include tiger worms, red wrigglers and Indian blues. You can buy these earthworms and their egg cocoons from commercial farms.

LEECHES

These little suckers are after your blood. They lurk in the leaf litter and damp vegetation, just waiting for you to brush past or pause within crawling range.

Leeches are the earthworms' creepy cousins. If you look closely, you can see the family resemblance. They're both long and thin and appear to be divided into rings. But where earthworms have pointy or rounded ends that help them burrow in soil, leeches have suckers for holding on tight while they're having lunch.

And they're good at holding on. If a leech is on the move, you can flick it away. But once it has settled down to dine, it can be very difficult to dislodge. Not only do they hang on with both suckers but they are also slimy and soft. The phrase 'stuck like a leech' is exactly right.

When feeding, the rear sucker keeps the leech in place, whereas the front one forms a seal against your skin. What you can't see—and usually don't feel—are the two or three saw-toothed jaws slicing into you. As the tiny blood vessels in your skin spill their contents, the leech pumps the liquid lunch into its digestive system. They are leisurely feeders and may take 20 minutes or more to fill up. By that time they've expanded to accommodate the meal. Because dinner is not a regular occurrence for blood feeders, they take as much as they can whenever they can.

How do they stay on for so long without letting you know they're about? After all, something as small as a black fly (p. 104) or mosquito (p. 107) gives the game away pretty quickly. Leeches are light and move slowly, so you usually don't feel them against your skin. Moreover, a leech is a complete surgical team in one little slippery unit. Having located a suitable feeding spot, a leech releases saliva that contains a complex mixture of medications. A local anaesthetic numbs your skin, so there's no sensation as the bladed jaws begin their incisions. A vasodilator opens up your blood vessels to ensure free flow and an anti-coagulant prevents clotting. Gruesome? Yes, but also remarkable.

When finished, the leech drops off, leaving a small wound that will keep on bleeding for a while longer.

Pal or pest?

How do I deal with them?

Insect repellent on shoes, socks and pants will deter them. An attached leech is difficult to dislodge. You might be able to remove it by sliding your fingernail under to break the grip. If that doesn't work, try spraying it with insect repellent, sprinkling it with table salt or dabbing on a few drops of tea tree oil or vinegar. Don't yank at the leech because that could cause the skin to tear.

Remember that the bite will continue to bleed for some time after the leech has been removed but will eventually stop. Wash the wound with soap and water and apply an antiseptic.

FLATWORMS

Flat, smooth and sticky. Although not familiar to most gardeners, you can easily recognise a few species. The shovel-headed worm has a brownish, striped body up to 20 cm long and—no surprises here!—a head resembling a shovel. The blue flatworm is 10 cm or less, with a tapering head and an inky-blue back with a pale stripe down the middle. Other common flatworms are brown or black, with a stripe or two.

Even though you might not see then very often, flatworms are common and widespread in gardens along the east coast. They live in compost heaps, under stones and logs and among the dead leaves. Because they're at risk of dehydrating, they don't come out when the humidity is low.

They are slow-moving predators that feed on equally slow-moving prey. Especially fond of earthworms, they glue down their wriggly dinner with sticky spit. Not only does the saliva tangle up the prey but also starts to digest it before it gets close to the flatworm's insides. Marinated earthworm, anyone?

Pal or pest?

Flatworms can be real pests if they get into earthworm farms. They will make a meal of the stock and finish them off in no time.

How do I deal with them?

Direct action is effective. Try laying out a wet sack or carpet square on the ground to make a desirable residence for flatworms. Once located, squash them or drop them into salty water. Wear gloves because the mucus may irritate bare skin.

MAGGOTS

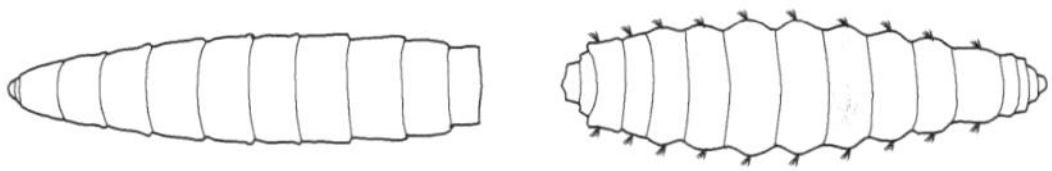

Maggots (fly larvae) are small, white or yellow crawlers that are usually tapered at one end and broad at the other. The broad end is marked with a pair of dots, which are the openings through which a maggot takes in air while its head is buried in food. So they breathe through the bum end . . . which is a good idea, considering what maggots prefer to eat: dead animals, poo and rotting vegies. If it's off, they like it. If it's putrid, they love it.

Maggots hatch from eggs laid directly onto their food. They remain with it, eating and growing bigger, until they are ready to change into flies. Because they are unable to escape from danger while transforming, they first wriggle away to locate a safe place to undergo the process. During this exodus, maggots may pop up anywhere. Sometimes they appear a long way from their site of origin.

Pal or pest?

Most maggots feed on rotting matter, doing that dirty but essential job of garbage disposal. Without them, we'd be stepping over piles of dead things. So—technically—they are pals, but they're the sort of the pals you'd prefer to keep at arm's length. The problem is not so much the maggots as their lunch.

How do I deal with them?

Prevention is much, much better than the cure. Cover or bury garbage to stop flies laying their eggs on it. No flies = no eggs = no maggots.

CHERRY OR PEAR SLUGS

Despite the name, they are not slugs at all but the slimy young of a type of sawfly. They coat themselves in gunk, which makes them look like . . . well . . . something sneezed out of your nose.

When they are about to turn into adults, cherry slugs shed their gummy covering. At this stage they are about 1 cm long and look like fat, yellow caterpillars. They migrate down the tree trunk and bury themselves in the soil at its base, where they spend weeks changing into adult sawflies.

Cherry slugs prefer cherry, pear, plum, quince and almond trees, but will live on other plants. They feed on leaves. At first, they chew at the surface, which makes the leaves look as though they've been scorched by the sun. As the grubs grow, they eat all the way through, sparing only the tough veins. A heavy infestation can reduce leaves to skeletons in no time at all.

Pal or pest?

One or two won't eat much but if they occur in large numbers, cherry slugs can be pests.

How do I deal with them?

For small numbers, pick them off by hand and squash them or knock them down with a squirt of water. Sprinkling wood ash over leaves will reduce larger infestations. Cultivating the soil around the tree or letting chooks loose in the area might prevent the cherry slugs from turning into adults and so break the cycle.

SPITFIRES

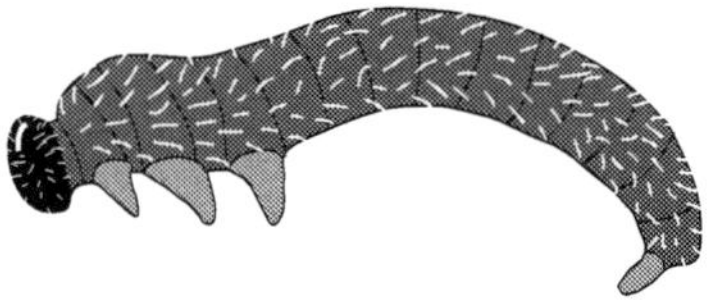

Have you seen a platoon of large, hairy grubs marching in close formation from one tree to another? Are they waving their rear ends in a menacing fashion and gobbing khaki-coloured goo when you get too close? Yes? Then you've got spitfires. Like cherry slugs (p. 23), they're the young of a sawfly.

Spitfires are common in gum trees over spring and summer. They feed on gum leaves, which contain an oil produced by the tree to discourage plant eaters. Not only can they cope with this oil, but they can also recycle it. As the insect munches away on a leaf, it separates the liquid from the edible parts and stores it in a special pouch near the mouth. If something gets too close—barf! They might have bad table manners and look alarming but spitfires are harmless to people.

Pal or pest?
Large groups of spitfires can strip all the leaves from a young tree.

How do I deal with them?

Because they cluster together during the day, it's a simple matter to snip off the twig or small branch and drop the insects into a bucket of hot water. Remember to dispose of them thoughtfully. Perhaps you could use them as compost.

Soap spray and pyrethrum-based insecticides are also effective, but the cheapest and driest way of dealing with the problem is to dust the larvae with wood ash. It's bad news for the insects but does no damage to the tree.

CATERPILLARS

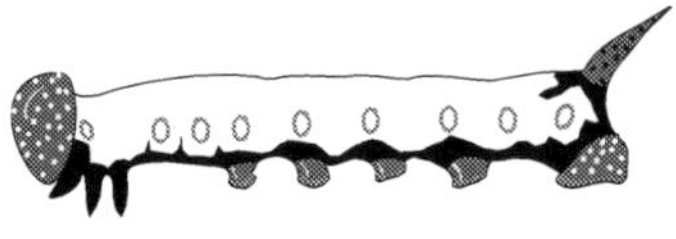

Hawk moth caterpillar

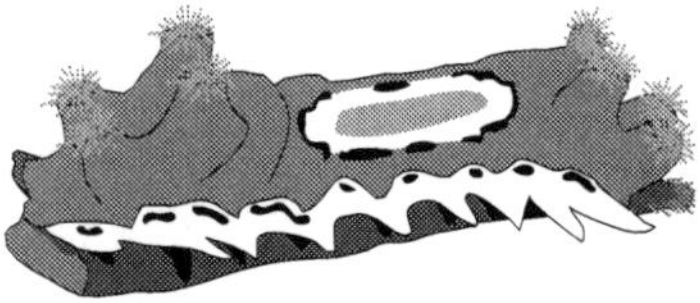

Cup moth caterpillar

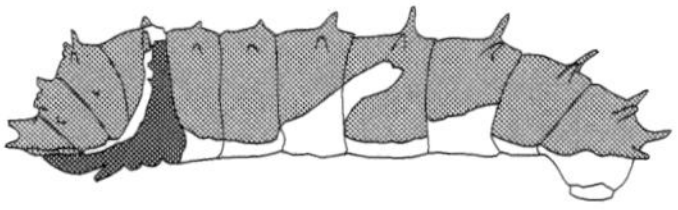

Orchard butterfly

If your garden is losing leaves to unseen diners, it might be suffering from a case of caterpillars. These little grubs will eventually transform into nectar-drinking butterflies and moths but, at this early stage of their lives, they're leaf-eating machines. And the garden is their buffet.

Butterflies and moths come in all shapes and colours (p. 112), so it's not surprising that their caterpillars are just as diverse. Despite the range, the youngsters have one thing in common—three pairs of true legs at the front end and up to five pairs of prolegs towards the rear. True legs are small and composed of segments (like those of other insects), whereas the prolegs are dumpy. The proleg quota is the easiest way of distinguishing caterpillars from beetle larvae (which have none). Telling caterpillars from sawfly larvae is another matter.

Look under leaves for these critters because they like to feed away from view. Some come out only at night, so you may have to go exploring with a torch. They're not always easy to spot. Apart from being secretive, many are coloured green or brown, so are well camouflaged against their dinner. Others are more exuberant because they've got in-built defences against predators. Caterpillars of orchard butterflies start life looking like bird poo but change into a more presentable green and white version as they grow. When frightened, they extend a Y-shaped structure from a pocket behind the head. The pong that comes along with it puts off most predators. Who wants to eat anything that smells like that?

Wanderer butterfly caterpillars are not only out and about in broad daylight but are also candy-striped in black, white and yellow. You'd think that would be asking for trouble. But the caterpillars are advertising that they're loaded with poisons. Cup moth caterpillars take it one step further. They're also brightly coloured—in lolly pink and yellow—but are armed with eight bunches of stinging hairs that cause pain on contact. A few common species of caterpillars are almost completely covered with bristles that sting and itch. Sometimes you don't see these until you've brushed against them.

Pal or pest? **Both**

One or two are not a problem but large numbers can be pests.

How do I deal with them?

Fine-meshed net keeps adults from laying eggs on vegies. If this is not practical, try spraying leaves with a mixture of garlic and water. This works as a repellent, discouraging caterpillars from feeding on the leaves.

Small numbers are easily contained by picking them off by hand. Squash them or donate them to the chooks. (Don't feed hairy or brightly coloured caterpillars to the poultry.)

Spraying plants with Bt (*Bacillus thuringiensis*) is an effective organic control (p. 217). This method targets leaf-eating caterpillars and has little impact on other species. Caterpillars stop feeding almost immediately and usually die within a few days.

Encouraging natural predators is a longer-term solution to keeping pest species under control. Other insects, spiders, lizards and small birds all feed on caterpillars.

INDIAN MEAL MOTH CATERPILLARS

They lurk in the darkness of the pantry. You don't notice the Indian meal moth caterpillars as they chew their way through your cereal and poo all over the pasta. It's not until you pour them out into your breakfast bowl and watch them crawl away from the light that you realise the awful truth. They've taken over the kitchen. And they're in *everything*.

They spend most of their time living in their dinner. When they are ready to turn into moths, they leave the cereal and crawl up the cupboard walls. They tuck themselves into corners and sit quietly while they make the transformation. Stop 'em when you can.

Pal or pest?

How do I deal with them?

Prevention is better than the cure with these moths. Once they've become established, it takes a lot of hard work to eradicate them. When buying bulk dry goods (cereal, dried beans, nuts, flour, pasta, rice . . . you get the picture), check the packages to make sure there's no sign of infestation. Usually this manifests itself as a collection of small, brownish granules (caterpillar poo) that look different from the rest of the product. Often this poo is caught up in small webs.

Even if a new purchase looks pest free, it's worth freezing it for a couple of days to kill any eggs. Store food in containers with tight-fitting snap-on lids because the little so-and-sos can squeeze between the threads on screw-top jars.

See p. 213 for information on controlling adult moths.

CABBAGE MOTH AND CABBAGE WHITE BUTTERFLY CATERPILLARS

If you've ever tried to grow cabbages or cauliflowers, radishes or rocket, you'll have almost certainly bumped into caterpillars of the cabbage moth and cabbage white butterfly. They don't look like much—they're both small, leaf green grubs—but their modest appearance is misleading. These little eating engines will chew their way through your vegie patch without hesitation.

Both species are so well camouflaged against their food

plant that you might not know about them until you see their handiwork—chewed leaves and piles of poo (frass). If you want to work out which species are ravaging your cabbages, check out the caterpillars' back ends. The moth often holds out its last two 'legs' (prolegs; see the general entry on caterpillars on p. 26) in a V-shape, whereas the butterfly caterpillar keeps them tucked under its bum.

Moth caterpillars also seal themselves into cocoons on the host plant, often among the florets of broccoli and cauliflowers. These shelters are enclosed in a fine net of silk, which looks better than it tastes. (Surprise!) Butterfly caterpillars leave the plant when they're about to change; but they leave behind a holey cabbage and a pile of poo.

Pal or pest?

How do I deal with them?

Pick them off by hand or use the caterpillar-specific spray Bt (p. 217). Try to get them while they are still feeding on the outer leaves. Once they work their way into the cabbage and cauliflower hearts they are protected from sprays.

BEETLE LARVAE

Wireworm

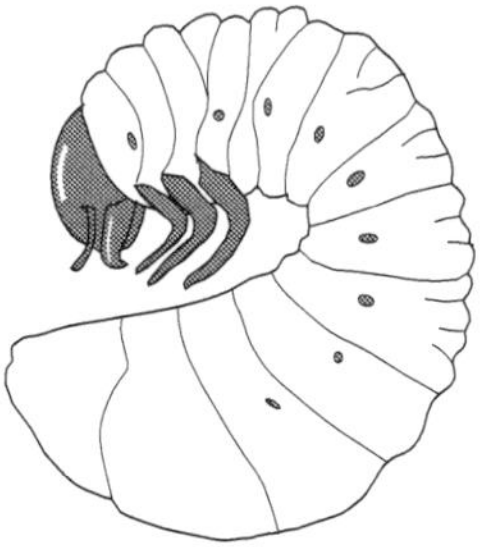

Curl grub scarab

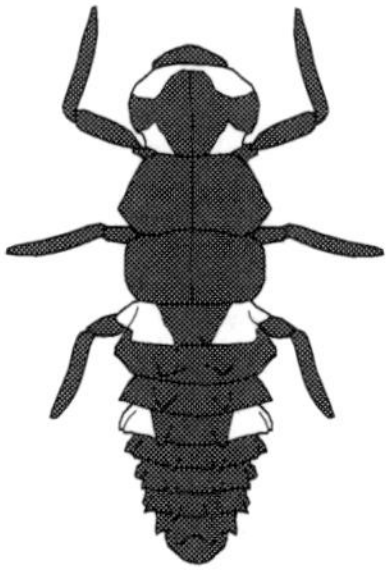

Ladybird larva

Have you ever stuck a shovel into the compost heap and uncovered a critter that looks like a chubby, white comma? Or picked up a plant pot and spotted a shiny brown grub crawling away? What about those tiny, spiky husks caught on the sofa cushions? Have you noticed those and wondered what's been living in the upholstery?

Beetles. Young 'uns. That's what.

Like butterflies and moths, beetles go through different stages as they grow—from egg to larva to adult. The larval stage looks more like a caterpillar than a full-grown beetle but you can tell the two apart by counting their legs. Beetle larvae have three pairs of legs immediately behind the head and nothing resembling legs anywhere beyond that (although there might be a structure for gripping right at the very end). Caterpillars also have the standard three pairs but possess up to an additional five pairs of prolegs towards the rear.

Because of the huge number of different beetles, identifying larvae to species can be tricky. Here are some clues to narrow the options.

Scarabs, cockchafers and Christmas beetles have fat white larvae that curl into a C-shape. (They're also known as curl grubs after this characteristic habit.) One of the largest is the rhinoceros beetle of northern Australia, which is over 4 cm long. Most are much smaller. Curl grubs usually live in soil, where they feed on plant roots. You may not even know they're around until the lawn turns into a patchwork of dying grass.

Longicorn larvae look like uncooked crinkle-cut fried chips. They live inside trees—living or dead, depending on the beetle species—and chew away at the wood. They're not the only ones to take up residence in this habitat. A whole range of borers spend their early lives eating their way through timber.

Click beetles and darkling beetles have lively larvae that resemble pale brown millipedes.

Ladybird larvae are predators that roam over leaves in search of aphids and other small insects. They are covered in spikes and spines. Like the adults, they're coloured black and yellow or black and orange. The colours are a warning to anything that might want to eat them—ladybirds young and old are full of poisons.

Pal or pest?

That depends on the species.

Curl grubs can be pests in large numbers because of the damage they inflict on lawns. Ladybird larvae are pals because they feed on sap-sucking insects. Identify your beetles first to work out how to treat them.

How do I deal with them?

Chemicals are available for controlling curl grubs but natural methods are probably best. Curl grubs seem to be everyone's favourite food. Magpies, currawongs and bandicoots love them. Soaking the ground brings the grubs to the surface, where the feathered and furred locals can get to them with less lawn-destroying effort.

By avoiding chemicals, you'll give ladybirds and other small predators a chance to do their thing.

MILLIPEDES

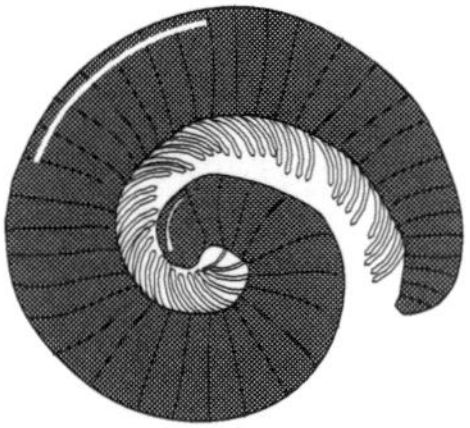

You've probably seen them in your bathroom, trundling across the floor or resting in little black question marks on the wall tiles. Millipedes are long, shiny and black with lots of short legs. And by lots, I mean two pairs to each segment, which adds up to hundreds of legs in the more extended models. The segments are flattish or, more commonly, curved on top like old-fashioned train carriages.

Millipedes live in mulch and under logs, stones and plant pots. They often wander into houses where you may see them marching determinedly across the floor. When disturbed, most species curl up. The pill millipede rolls into a ball by tucking its head under its backside. Some types of millipedes release a pongy fluid that puts off predators. It may stain your skin yellow or red but won't harm you—unless you swallow it, so always wash your hands after handling them.

The introduced Portuguese millipede occasionally occurs in plague proportions. Swarms have held up trains because the wheels couldn't grip on the slimy, squashed mess.

Pal or pest?

Are millipedes marching all over the garden and/or house? Pest.

How do I deal with them?

If they're where they shouldn't be, relocate them to the compost heap, either before or after squashing them. Because millipedes have difficulty crawling up smooth surfaces, a wall of plastic tape may keep them out of the house. If you try this, make sure the barrier is 50 mm or more in height to prevent them climbing over it.

CENTIPEDES

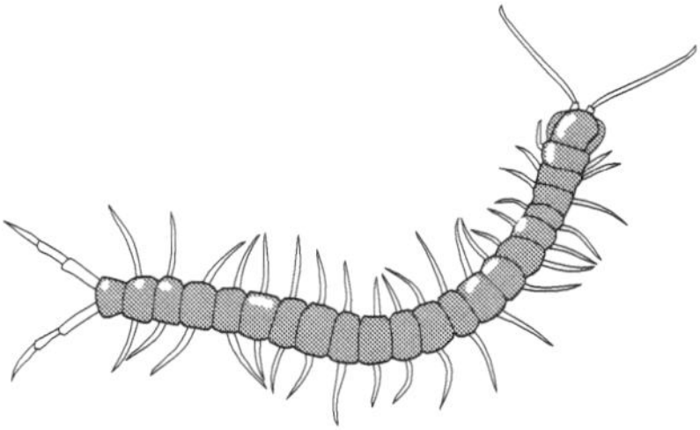

Centipedes are long, flat, yellow, grey or brown critters with an abundance of legs that stick out to the side like oars. Most garden centipedes are small, but some tropical and inland species are giants (15 cm or more). They can move very quickly.

Centipedes have a pair of antennae and two curved poison-injecting claws, which they tuck away under the head. The last two legs are held off the ground, giving the impression of pincers.

Generally, centipedes all look pretty much the same, but house centipedes are nonconformists. They have short bodies, thread-like antennae and fifteen pairs of long legs. If you see something that looks like a false eyelash scuttling across the floor, it's probably one of these.

Did I mention they move very quickly?

Most centipedes live in the mulch and under stones and logs. They will also hide under loose bark on gum trees.

House centipedes often wander into homes, where they take up residence in bathrooms and basements.

Centipedes feed on insects, earthworms and other invertebrates, which they dispatch with fast-acting venom injected through the tips of their poison claws. Once dinner is ready, centipedes either slice it up or suck out the juices. They excel at cleaning up garden pests.

Pal or pest?
In the garden? Pal.
In the house? Pest.

How do I deal with it?

Always check your shoes before sticking your feet into them, especially if you've left them outside. If you're bitten by a large centipede, watch for signs of an allergic reaction (p. 223).

VELVET WORMS

If you own a bush block in the wetter parts of the east coast, you might be sharing your garden with these weird little beasts. Looking like a cross between an earthworm (p. 14) and a millipede (p. 35), they're the descendants of a group of animals that originated more than 550 million years ago. Way back then, they all lived in the ocean. Now, there are no marine velvet worms: all live on land.

The common name comes from the texture of their skin—soft and covered in tiny bumps. In some species, the bumps are coloured in muted shades of yellow, brown and grey. Under a magnifying glass, these velvet worms look as though they're wrapped in Persian carpets.

Because of their size (a few centimetres) and their habitat (inside rotting logs), velvet worms are easy to overlook. Although small, they're big-time predators, hunting down termites and other small prey. What they lack in bulk, they make up in fancy accessories. Instead of chasing down dinner, they squirt it with glue. Then they can dine at leisure, partially dissolving their victims with saliva and chopping up the remainder with their sharp jaws.

If that's not odd enough, you should hear about their mating habits. But we've run out of space.

Pal or pest?

How do I deal with them?

If your backyard is big enough, leave fallen timber to provide a home for them. They seem to prefer logs that are so rotten you can tear them apart with bare hands.

HOPPERS, SKIPPERS AND JUMPERS

GRASSHOPPERS, LOCUSTS AND KATYDIDS

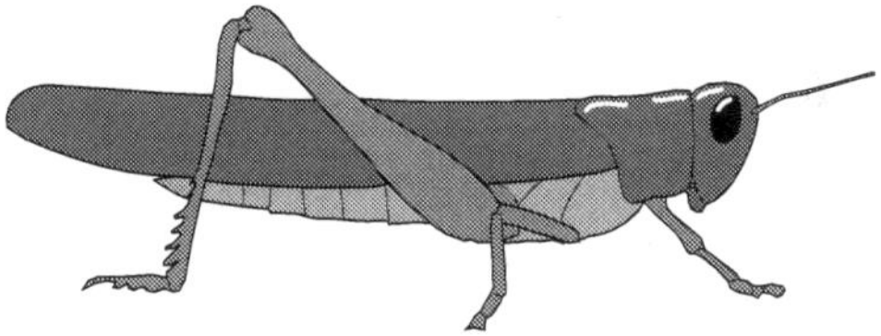

Grasshopper

In summer, grasshoppers and katydids sit in the sun and sing romantic melodies to woo the girls. Listen closely and you'll hear different pitches and rhythms in their tunes. Each species has its own call.

But this advertising also makes it easy for predators to find them, so they rely on camouflage to disappear among the grass and bushes. If you get too close to a grasshopper, it will spring into the air and land . . . somewhere. Those leaps are powered by long, powerful hind legs.

For grasshoppers and locusts the hind legs do double duty both as an escape mechanism and a musical instrument. (And you can't say that about many things.) They draw the legs across the front pair of wings to make buzzes and trills. Katydids rub their wings together to play their melodies.

Grasshoppers and locusts feed on plant leaves and shoots, causing problems when they swarm in big numbers. Katydids have a wider diet, including plant pollen and other insects. They're less likely to gather together, so will have a lower impact on your garden.

Pal or pest?
Pests in large numbers.

How do I deal with them?

It isn't easy to control grasshoppers. Their leaping and flying skills make them difficult to catch by hand or even with a net. If you want to try it, go after them early in the morning before they've livened up.

Insect sprays will cause collateral damage, affecting the beneficial Spineless as well as the troublemakers. Instead, try deterrents like garlic sprays and encourage insect-eating birds, frogs, lizards, wasps and spiders into the garden. They'll jump at the chance . . . *sorry.*

LANDHOPPERS

Have you ever raked up fallen leaves and seen a bunch of small grey or brown animals spring off the ground like oversized fleas? They're landhoppers, the energetic cousins of slaters (p. 98). Close up, they look like their more sedate relatives . . . that have been squashed in a vice. And just like slaters, their next of kin live in the ocean. (Turn over seaweed at the high tide line to see the marine version. They skip around just as enthusiastically as the garden-dwellers.)

Those hoppers in your garden are only *barely* land animals. They live in leaf litter so damp it's almost under water. Where conditions are suitable, they occur in very high densities—hundreds of hoppers per square metre—but are usually found in much lower numbers. They chew up dead and decaying plants, returning nutrients to the soil in their poo.

Under a magnifying glass, landhoppers are all limbs and antennae. Their seven pairs of legs have specialised functions. (The Swiss Army knife of the animal world?) The last three pairs are set up for leaping. They don't power the jump but balance the spring-loaded animal as it readies for action. The leap itself is powered by the sudden straightening out of the curled body. Although they don't know where they're going to land, neither do predators—a haphazard but handy escape mechanism.

Pal or pest?

Unless landhoppers are at plague levels, they're pals.

How do I deal with them?

They are vulnerable to drying out, so rake up and dispose of damp leaf litter if you're having problems with a load of landhoppers.

FLEAS

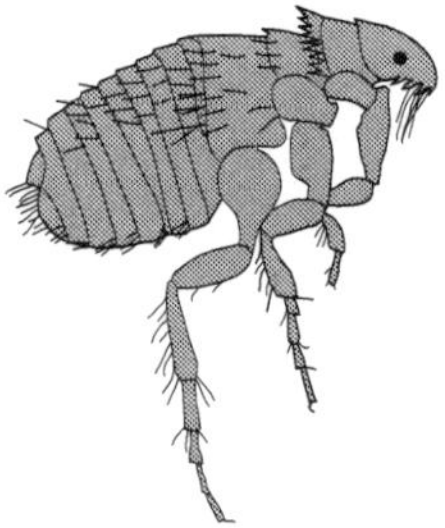

Often the first signs of fleas about the place are itchy bite marks on your bare ankles. If you manage to glance down at the right moment, you'll see a small dark oval attached to your skin. A close look reveals an adult flea, only a couple of millimetres long and flattened from side to side like a squashed apple pip. When disturbed, fleas jump using their long hind legs. Those legs can propel them about 30 cm straight up and 20 cm thataway. Sure, they don't know where they're going to land, but neither do you. It's a very effective way to escape.

Adult fleas are bloodsuckers. Unlike leeches, they don't have a local anaesthetic in their saliva. When they bite, you feel it. And then—to add insult to (minor) injury—their spit causes a maddening itch. Not that the larvae have better table manners. These tiny worm-like critters live in carpets and pet bedding, where they feed on skin flakes and similar substances. At all stages of their lives, fleas are dependent on other animals for their food.

To make matters worse, fleas can also transmit tapeworms to dogs. Young fleas pick up worm eggs when they nibble on dog poo. The worms hatch and develop inside the fleas—a parasite within a parasite. When the dog accidentally swallows infected fleas while grooming itself, the tapeworms settle down for a cosy life inside Spot's intestine. Unfortunately, tapeworm eggs can infect us too. I'm not going to draw a picture but be careful if Spot licks you . . .

Pal or pest?
Are you kidding? Pests. Definitely.

How do I deal with them?

Flea control requires a major effort. Even if you think you've beaten the adults, eggs and larvae may still be lurking in your carpet. Then, after a few weeks of flea-free bliss, the itching starts all over again.

The trick is to interrupt the cycle. Vacuuming carpets and pet beds and blankets reduces the eggs and larvae. If the infestation is heavy, you may need to vacuum daily for a couple of weeks. (Yes, I know. That makes me shudder too, but vacuuming is a lot better than hosting fleas.)

Adult fleas are difficult to catch. If you have tolerant pets, try grooming them with a fine-tooth comb. Fleas tend to congregate around the neck or tummy, but can be found anywhere furry. Once you've dislodged them with the comb, you have to act quickly. Wet your finger tips and squeeze the insect. Water slows them down a bit because it gums up their back legs. (Once they jump, you've lost them.) What you do with your captive flea is up to you. Dunking them in warm soapy water is a good way of disposing of them.

A vet can recommend flea treatments for your pet. You might consider regular worming too. Of pets, that is.

Break the cycle. Fleas are *very* persistent.

EIGHT-LEGGED CRAWLERS

SPIDERS

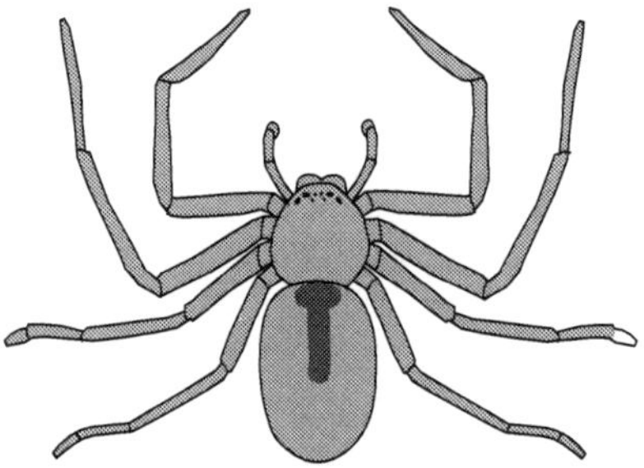

Spiders have suffered bad press over the years. Despite all the good they do in keeping down pest insects, we tend to focus on the unpleasant aspects of a few species. I blame Little Miss Muffet.

Spiders come in a variety of shapes and sizes, from tiny money spiders to spindly daddy-long-legs to hulking, hairy funnel-webs, but they all share certain characteristics. They have four pairs of legs, multiple eyes (usually eight but occasionally only six) and a body divided into two parts. This last feature distinguishes spiders from those other eight-legged Spineless that you might spot around the house and garden. Of course, that means getting up close to check . . . Near enough might be good enough.

Australia is home to thousands of species of spiders but only a small proportion of those are frequent visitors to your garden. An even smaller fraction will make it into your house. Many of the more common drop-ins are easy to identify.

Huntsman spiders are probably the most familiar of the house-callers. These large, flattish critters normally live under bark or in rock crevices, coming out at night to hunt insects and other invertebrates. Your walls are much the same to them as tree trunks or cliff faces. A domestic huntsman will spend its evening patrolling the house on the lookout for a meal and then find a quiet retreat at dawn. Unfortunately, that quiet retreat is often a fold in a curtain or the back of a sofa cushion, resulting in a big surprise for all parties involved.

Daddy-long-legs are also willing to share our sheds and houses. Spinning their tatty webs in quiet corners, they trap moths, flies and other household pests. Daddy-long-legs are also partial to other spiders—including redbacks—which they tangle in silk threads before their victims have a chance to fight back. This skill has led to the mistaken belief that they are the most venomous spiders of all and could kill you with a single bite if only their jaws were big enough to get through your skin. Daddy-long-legs' venom is mild and unlikely to cause anything more than a local reaction (if even that).

White-tailed spiders are wanderers, often strolling into houses on the lookout for food or mates. They're not difficult to identify—their elongated abdomens end in the white spot that gives the spiders their common name. Despite their reputation, there's no reliable evidence that white-tail bites cause anything other than a local reaction in people. But it's not the same story for other spiders, when white-tails sink in the fangs. White-tails are spider-hunters, pouncing on their eight-legged prey, injecting venom and dining at leisure. Now there's a dilemma for arachnophobes: are white-tailed spiders pals or pests?

Black house spiders build their untidy webs under window sills, in gaps in masonry and other tight spots around the house and garden. The web is tunnel-shaped with a tangle of threads spreading out from the entrance. It does double duty as a cosy retreat and a snare for insects. From the security of the tunnel mouth, the owner keeps eight eyes on what's happening outside. If food ambles within striking range, the spider darts out to catch it. If a predator passes by, the spider scuttles the other way.

Redback spiders have taken to humans in a big way. They construct their webs in wood piles, on fences, in the shed and garage and under garden furniture. Rarely leaving their messy home, they usually come into direct contact with us only when we inadvertently shove our hands into a web. It's only not surprising that a redback might react with a swift and painful bite. You'd probably do the same if the roles were reversed. Only female redbacks sport the characteristic scarlet blaze on a glossy black background. Males are brown with white markings on the back and a pale 'hourglass' underneath.

Funnel-web spiders and other large ground-dwelling spiders (including mouse spiders, trapdoor spiders and wishbone spiders) may take up residence in your garden. Although most of them prefer to stay in the safety of their burrows, males, in particular, go a-wandering to look for mates. Sydney funnel-webs pack the most dangerous venom, which can be a problem when they live so close to people.

Wolf spiders are also ramblers. You might disturb a few of these long-legged, fast movers when you're gardening. It's easy to underestimate the number of them on your lawn. Here's something for the non-arachnophobes to do on a warm summer night. Go outside with a torch. Hold it up level to your eyes and shine it over the lawn. See those little blue-green sparkles in the grass? That's not dew. That's the reflection from the eyes of wolf spiders. (You can try this trick on tree bark to locate huntsmen.) Now imagine how many insects they clean up in a day.

Orb weavers are homebodies. They construct elaborate wheel-shaped webs to catch flying insects. These snares can be huge—up to two metres across in the case of the golden orb weaver. They often wait at the centre of the web, from where they can dash out to wrap up dinner when it blunders in. Garden orb weavers often build the web anew each night, dismantling it in the morning. Others—the candy-striped St Andrew's cross spider and golden orb weaver among them—construct permanent webs.

Pal or pest?
Pal, mostly, but watch out for funnel-web and redback spiders about the house and garden.

How do I deal with them?

If a spider is indoors and you'd prefer it to be somewhere else, you can relocate is using the jar and card method (p. 207). This works best with smaller spiders. You may have to use a clear plastic lunchbox or other container for huntsmen.

Orb weavers often build their webs in just the wrong

place—across paths, on clotheslines or children's play equipment. If this is a problem, try breaking the web every time it appears. The spider will get the message and move somewhere quieter. Be careful not to stick your fingers where the web owner can nip them because orb weaver bites can be unpleasant (but not dangerous).

Bites from redback and funnel-web spiders are a different story. Although many redback bites result in nothing worse than local pain and nausea, always take them seriously. Funnel-web bites are medical emergencies. Anti-venom is available for both redback and funnel-web bites. For more information on first aid for spider bites, see p. 226.

HARVESTMEN

At first glance, they look very similar to spiders—rounded bodies, eight long legs, making themselves at home under plant pots . . . But a closer examination reveals differences. Whereas a spider's body is clearly divided into two parts joined by a narrow waist, a harvestman's body is chunkier. The two parts appear fused into a single element. Another clue is the relative lengths of the legs. The second pair is longer and thinner than the other three pairs and is used to detect what's lying ahead and to the sides, in much the same way that cockroaches use their antennae.

If you take an even closer look, perhaps with a magnifying glass Sherlock Holmes-style, you might see the harvestman peering back at you out of two eyes, not six or eight. It might have a surprised expression. After all, most people don't pay that much attention to them.

Harvestmen are common in gardens but are easy to miss. Although not particularly secretive, they are small and live under logs and rocks and in mulch. They prefer locations that are moist and sheltered and provide a steady supply of food. Unlike spiders, which are exclusively carnivorous, harvestmen have broad diets. They will eat just about anything, including dead animals and bird poo.

Pal or pest?

Pal. They clean up the waste. (Not as efficiently as maggots, of course, but with more finesse.)

How do I deal with them?

Provide plenty of hiding places to encourage them to stay.

SCORPIONS

Scorpions may be small animals—many are no longer than your little finger—but they pack a wallop. Although related to spiders and ticks, the family resemblance isn't all that strong. A scorpion has a long, flat, segmented body with a pair of claws at one end and a tail at the other. Those claws can crush insects into submission, but the tail is the business end as far as we're concerned. It carries a thorn-like sting, which is loaded with venom. When upset, a scorpion will raise its tail to bring the sting into striking position. Although they don't go looking for trouble, preferring to retreat if possible, they will use the sting if pressed.

The venom of Australian scorpions is painful but not dangerous to humans. (I can vouch for this.)

Although you don't see them very often, scorpions are more common than you might expect. They spend the day under rocks and loose bark. In drier areas, they live in burrows. At night, they emerge to hunt for insects. Their wanderings may bring them into houses and sheds, where they'll look for somewhere to hide during the day.

Pal or pest?

They're pals *outside* the house.

How do I deal with them?

If a scorpion wanders in, use the jar and card technique to capture it for relocation to somewhere more suitable.

Don't panic if you're stung. Get medical attention if there are any signs of allergic reactions (p. 223).

MITES

Those eight-legged full stops crawling across your rose leaves are mites. Unless you're wielding a magnifying glass, all mites look pretty much the same. The exceptions are red velvet mites, which are eyecatching in the way that any crawling, crimson, plush-piled punctuation marks draw attention.

Although there's not a great deal of diversity in their appearance, there's plenty of it in their lifestyles. Mites live everywhere—on land, in rivers and lakes and in the sea. They nosh on plants by sucking out sap from leaves and flowers. Some feed on other tiny Spineless beings. Many species live on (and in) larger animals, including spiders, millipedes and snails. A few even tunnel into human skin, resulting in local reactions that include inflammation and severe itching.

Sap-sucking mites create serious problems in gardens. A heavy infestation of two-spotted spider mites causes leaf drop in fruit and vegetable plants. The telltale signs of this species are yellow mottling on the upper surface of leaves and a network of fine threads underneath.

Red-legged earth mites go after pea and bean seedlings. The common name says it all—they're dark fuzzy critters with scarlet legs—a striking combination on a microscopic scale. They're a big problem in crops but also infest vegie patches.

Citrus bud mites are too small to spot without a powerful magnifying glass but the results of their activities are obvious to the naked eye. Infested flower buds and fruit grow into bizarre shapes.

Predatory mites hunt down their sapsucking cousins and other small invertebrates, including fungus gnats and thrips (p. 87). Because of their diet, several species are bred commercially for use in controlling pests in greenhouses and market gardens. They can polish off 20 or more eggs or five adults a day. An impressive feat when you consider the relative sizes of meal and diner!

Mites don't restrict themselves to plants and other invertebrates. The diseases scabies and mange are caused by burrowing mites. They live in places where the skin is thin and easy to excavate. By eating skin cells, they hollow out tiny tunnels in which the females lay their eggs. A few mites don't create problems but when their numbers build, that's when the trouble starts. Itching and infection follow. If untreated, the situation can become severe. These mites spread by direct contact.

Pal or pest?

Predatory mites are pals.
Sapsucking and parasitic mites are pests.

How do I deal with them?

Control plant-eating mites in the garden with predatory mites (p. 216) or by spraying with white oil (p. 217). Remember that white oil will affect other Spineless, so use it sparingly.

Scabies infections are eradicated by a combination of topical treatment and by laundering clothes and bedding at high temperatures (50°C) to kill mites. Talk to your GP or pharmacist for detailed advice. Your vet will recommend treatment for mange in dogs. Take care of the problem as soon as you detect it.

TICKS

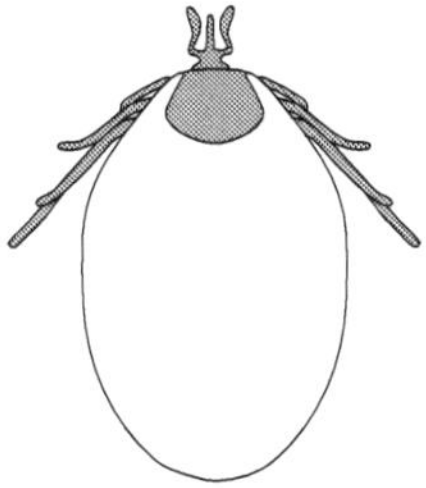

Ticks have eight dumpy legs and a squat, flat body that swells up when full of the favourite food—blood.

They look like overgrown mites. The resemblance is more than coincidental: the two are very closely related. It's easy to distinguish ticks from their smaller cousins, because the bloodsuckers have a small roundish or oblong plate (shield) at the head end and distinctive mouthparts. Those mouthparts are made up of a central tube (hypostome) adorned with backward-pointing barbs and two small feelers that sit on either side of it. When a tick feeds, it buries the mouthparts in skin. The barbs anchor it in place, making it difficult to detach a tick if it doesn't want to leave.

Ticks loiter on leaves and grass in damp areas until a suitable food source brushes past. Species that usually dine on the blood of kangaroos, bandicoots and other furry animals will also latch onto people. They're not fussy eaters.

They feed only three times during their lives—each time on a different individual. The final meal provides a female tick with enough energy to produce the next generation. Bloated with blood, she drops off her host and starts laying eggs. Thousands of them.

Ticks may transmit diseases from one host to the next. When feeding, they concentrate the nutritious parts of the blood by extracting unwanted water and salts from it and regurgitating them into the host. They can keep this up for days, if they're not removed. Their appalling table manners mean that other things might be injected with the discarded waste, including bacteria.

But bacteria aren't the biggest problem with tick bites in Australia. The saliva of the paralysis tick can cause a serious reaction in cats and dogs. If not treated quickly enough, the bite induces paralysis, starting with the hind legs and spreading forward. It may end in death. Paralysis tick poison also affects people but the impact is nowhere near as severe.

Pal or pest?

Their mothers might love them but there's nothing nice about ticks from a host's point of view.

How do I deal with them?

When in tick country, wear a broad-brimmed hat, a long-sleeved top, long trousers and shoes and socks. Cover exposed areas with insect repellent. Also spray repellent onto your shoes and waistband to deter ticks from finding a way through. Always check yourself and your pets after travelling through tick country. Ticks may settle in for a meal anywhere on your body, but they seem to be especially fond of armpits, groins and scalp. On returning, put your clothes in the washing machine and jump into the shower. That will take care of any ticks that have yet to settle in.

If possible, kill the tick with a human-safe pesticide, such as anti-scabies cream. (Repellents won't kill it.) This might take a few minutes. In many cases, the tick will drop off. If it doesn't, or if you have no suitable pesticide to hand, you will have to pull out the tick.

Tugging at it may remove the body but leave the mouthparts embedded in the skin. This is not a good outcome. Use a pair of tweezers to grasp the animal as close to the skin as possible. Pull it straight out. Don't twist. Don't yank. If the mouthparts stay behind, you may require medical attention to remove them or to treat allergic reactions to the saliva.

SIX-LEGGED CRAWLERS

ANTS

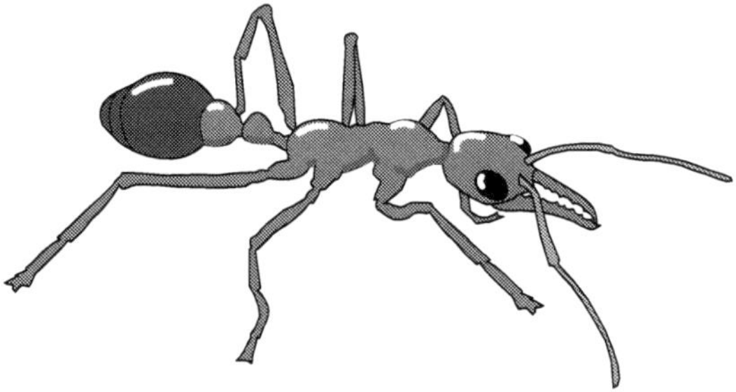

Ants are not shy, retiring insects. If they're around, you'll see them. (Or feel them, if you're too close to the nest.) Worker ants venture forth from the colony to search for food, which they carry back to support their nest mates. On finding a source, they lay down scent trails to guide others to the bounty. A lone ant is replaced by hundreds, diligently gathering food to feed the family at home. Unfortunately this anty altruism often involves them helping themselves to the contents of your kitchen or picnic hamper.

Colonies comprise from hundreds to thousands of individuals, which are grouped into different roles. Soldiers protect the nest from threats; workers collect food and look after the young; and one or more queen ants produce eggs to keep the colony going. At certain times of the year, winged ants leave to establish new colonies elsewhere.

There are thousands of species of ants in Australia. Unless you're a specialist, most of them look much the same. You can identify some of the more common ones from a combination of appearance, behaviour and nest type.

Green tree ants fasten together leaves to build nests in trees. (They use silk produced by larvae, which adults hold in their jaws and wield like glue-sticks.) Colonies can grow to a huge size, spreading over multiple nests in different trees. These little yellow and green ants are aggressive. When confronted with a threat (however mild), they bite and raise their abdomens to blast away with squirts of formic acid.

Bull ants and jack jumpers are big (sometimes more than 30 mm long) and belligerent. Their jaws are long, strong and capable of delivering a nasty bite. Once latched on to your skin, these ants also wield a sting that injects a cocktail of poisons. You can't miss the point. They have good eyesight, which they use to locate prey but also to track your movement if you get too close.

Meat ants build underground nests that are covered with low mounds of gravel or sand. (Don't stand on them!

The ants will bite.) A colony may occupy several nests. Workers are so large (up to 10 mm) and numerous that they tread down 'ant highways' where they commute between nests or to and from a reliable food source.

Fire ants are small, aggressive ants with a painful sting. Introduced from overseas in ships' cargo, they are currently restricted to southeastern Queensland. Their nests resemble those of meat ants but have no obvious entry holes.

Funnel ants also dig out underground nests. The openings to the nests are surrounded by a collar of sand or gravel, which protects them and may also help direct six-legged food straight into the larder.

Sugar ants are common around the house and garden. These ants love honeydew—the sweet secretions that leak from the rear ends of scale insects and aphids (p. 74)—and will protect the source from predators. (Other types of ants also do this, including meat and funnel ants.)

Introduced Argentine ants invade houses on the look-out for food and water. Unlike most other species, in which new colonies are founded far from the original, these tiny ants tend to stick close together. As the population grows, they move into fresh areas to build new nests but link them to the older ones. This means they can form supercolonies, sometimes *kilometres* in diameter, which take over the place and boot out native species. This has a knock-on effect for the animals that feed on those native ants. Add that to their house-invading tendencies and you can see why they are listed in the Top 100 of pest species.

Pharaoh ants are even smaller than Argentine ants. Also introduced (this time from West Africa), they are pests in houses and storage areas.

Pal or pest?

Ants are pests when they're in the house or in the wrong part of the garden. Because of their poisonous stings, bull ants and fire ants can be dangerous. If you discover fire ants on your property, notify your state Department of Primary Industries.

How do I deal with them?

Ants are persistent insects. Because of the sheer numbers in a nest, tackling a few foraging workers or soldiers won't have much of an impact on the rest. Practical methods for dealing with them depend on the size and location of the colony.

If ants have taken up residence among the roots of potted plants, submerge the pots in a bucket of water for at least 24 hours. Do this outside; otherwise you may end up with a mass of fleeing ants looking for a new home in your house.

Disturbing nests will eventually drive the ants elsewhere. It takes a great deal of effort to persuade them to move. Be prepared for a war of attrition—pitting your patience against their numbers. Ant baits act slowly but are thorough. Worker ants take them back to the nest, where everyone gets a share. You can deal with individual nests with boiling water or a bait mixed with diatomaceous earth (p. 214).

A compromise might be to dissuade them from foraging in your home by sprinkling lavender or eucalyptus oil around the entry. It confuses their scent trails and overwhelms their sense of smell.

Take care around bull ants and jack jumpers. If stung, watch for signs of allergic reactions. These are not to be taken lightly.

BEETLES

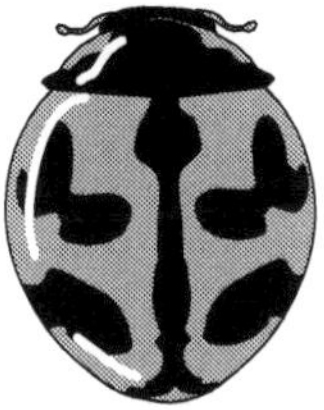

Ladybird

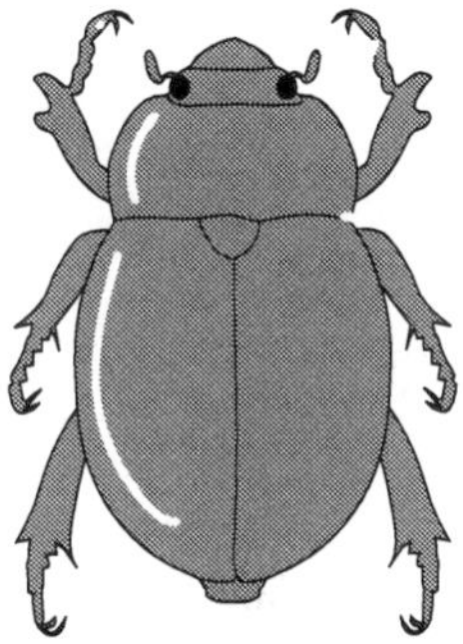

Christmas beetle

There are more types of beetles than any other type of animal. (Except, perhaps, nematode worms—but that's another story.) They vary in size from tiny critters than could waltz on pin heads to huge monsters up to 80 mm in length. Because of the variation, it is hard to give a description that covers them all. But here goes . . . A typical beetle possess a pair of wing covers (elytra) on its back. They meet in the middle, giving the impression of a groove running down the back. (It's not a brilliant description but it'll get you started.)

Like butterflies and moths (p. 112), beetles undergo a dramatic transformation from young to adult stages. Beetle larvae often look similar to caterpillars and it's easy to get them confused. You can find out more about the difference between them on p. 233.

Most beetles live in the great outdoors but a few thrive inside houses. Carpet beetles look like tiny brown and white mottled ladybirds. They hang around in floor coverings, upholstery and among clothes in cupboards and wardrobes. Drugstore beetles are small, dusty brown insects that tuck their heads under their bodies. They live in stored food. If you spot adults, watch out for their larvae.

Among the garden visitors, ladybirds are probably the most familiar. These red, orange or yellow and black glossy critters trundle over plants in search of aphids and other small pests. (Not all of them are good guys. A few species also dine on vegie leaves.) Some leaf beetles look similar to ladybirds but have longer antennae. They're not as helpful around the garden because of their diet. (You can work out what they eat.)

Scarabs, cockchafers and Christmas beetles are robust, ground-dwelling rounded beetles with strong legs for digging. Adults feed on leaves and flowers, whereas the larvae (curl grubs, p. 32) chew on plant roots in the soil.

Their cousins, the dung beetles, roll up poo into neat little balls and bury it in soil as food for their young. Native species specialise in marsupial poo and are overwhelmed by the volume produced by cattle and other domesticated animals. Dung beetles brought in from overseas do a great job of clearing up the output from large mammals. Councils use them to assist in reducing the problem of dog poo in parks.

Click beetles look as though they're hinged across the middle. If a beetle finds itself on its back, a simple but elegant mechanism involving a peg and a notch allows it to flip itself into the air. With luck, it will land the correct side up. If not, the beetle keeps clicking until it has got it right.

Weevils come in all sizes, colours and shapes but you can recognise them by their antennae, which are bent like an elbow, and their long snout (rostrum), which might be slender or chunky. One of the first Australian insects described was a weevil—Joseph Banks collected the metallic blue-green and black diamond weevil on wattles at Botany Bay.

Wood-chewing longicorn beetles are usually large beetles with long bodies and very long swept-back antennae. Auger, powderpost and ambrosia beetles are also fond of wood. These small, pellet-shaped insects burrow into timber, causing problems if they occur in large numbers.

Pal or pest?

Adult beetles feeding on wood or leaves can be pests.

How do I deal with them?

Adult beetles are tough to control. If they're in the garden, encourage predators—especially birds, frogs and lizards—to do the hard work for you. Inside the house, take care of carpet beetles by vacuuming regularly and washing or steamcleaning upholstery. Clothing, curtains and cushion covers can be wrapped up and popped into a freezer to kill adults and larvae. You'll have to leave them there for a week or more, to ensure that all stages are frozen. Drugstore beetles live in stored products. Prevent infestation by freezing dry goods for a few days before opening the packets. If the beetles have established themselves in your pantry, the easiest (if not cheapest) way to eliminate them is to get rid of the infested products.

Beetles that infest seasoned timber usually require professional attention. Painting timber can reduce infestation (or re-infestation, if they've already had a go).

BUGS

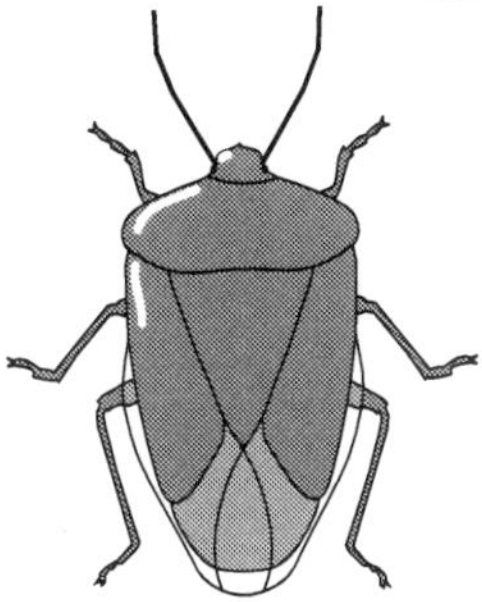

Stink bug

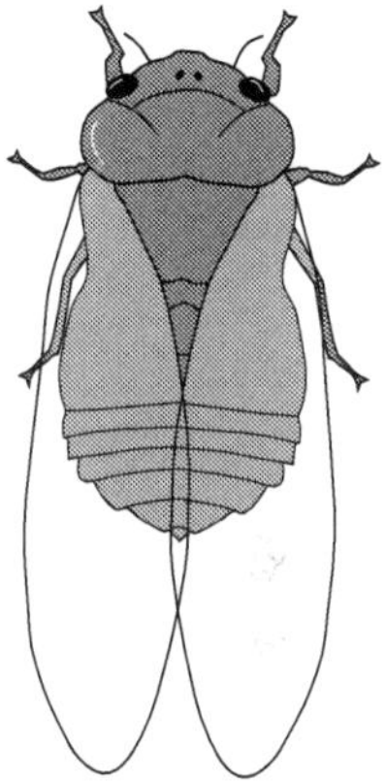

Cicada

We throw the name around and use it for any number of multi-legged critters, but 'bug' has a specific meaning in the Spineless world. It applies to a large group of insects with mouthparts adapted to feeding on liquids. Those liquids are mostly plant sap but may also be the body fluids of other insects. (Bugs are not above a little cannibalism.)

Bugs occur in a variety of forms. Although they don't look much like one another, cicadas, aphids (p. 74) and scale insects (p. 198) are all bugs. So are water boatmen and planthoppers. Unlike beetles, they don't go through a complete change in shape from young to adult. Baby bugs are small, wingless versions of the adults. They just get bigger with each moult.

The buzz of cicadas can be almost deafening in summer. Each species has its own song, produced by vibrating parts of the body over resonating chambers. Adults live in trees and bushes, where they feed on sap. Young cicadas spend years underground. When they are ready to become adults, they emerge from the soil and find a place to break out from their skin. In late spring, trees are festooned with the cast-off skins of young cicadas.

If you see thorns on a plant that shouldn't have them, take a closer look. Do the thorns move around to the other side of the stem? If so, they're planthoppers. (Or you're growing a triffid.)

Assassin bugs sit and wait for something tasty to amble past. They restrain their insect prey with their front legs and suck out its insides through their long tubular mouthparts. If you get on the wrong side of a large assassin bug, it won't hesitate to use those mouthparts on you too—but strictly in self-defence! Assassin bugs are easily recognised by their mouthparts, which are curved and clearly visible under the head.

Some shield bugs feed on plants, whereas others feed on insects. Many of them produce a unpleasant pong when attacked, which has given them the alternative name of stink bug.

Jewel bugs possess a hard covering over the wings, which make them look similar to beetles. If you look closely, you'll see that the covering is a single sheet, not two separate cases. This distinguishes them from ladybirds and other brightly coloured beetles. The vivid combinations of metallic blue, green and red make the harlequin bug unforgettable, especially when they're feeding on your hibiscus.

Pal or pest?
Plant-suckers can be pests, especially in vegie gardens. Insect-eaters are pals.

How do I deal with them?

You can pick off small numbers of bugs by hand and squash or drown them. Unfortunately, pest bugs often occur in large numbers. Pyrethrum-based sprays work on such big populations but will also kill other insects.

The pong given off by stink bugs deters others, so—if you can stand it—mix up some squashed bugs with warm water and use it as a spray. You may have to reapply this regularly because it dissipates rapidly.

Many animals eat bugs, including wasps and other bugs.

APHIDS

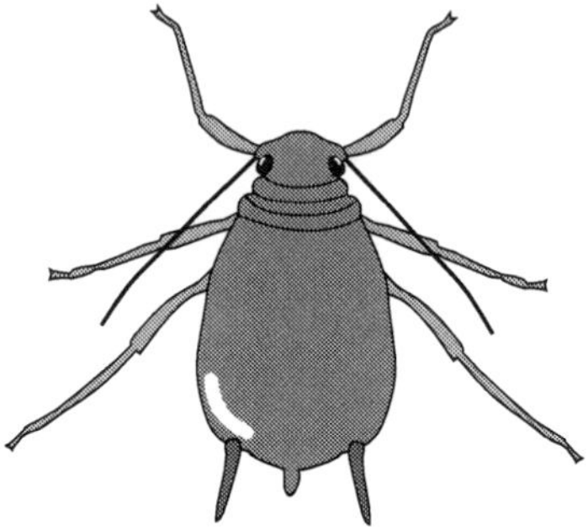

These tiny bugs cluster together on stems and under leaves. If you look closely, you might see a mixed bag of winged and wingless adults and young ones of different sizes. There's a lot going on in the aphid world.

They suck up plant sap. When feeding, they excrete a sticky fluid called honeydew. (Or aphid wee. Take your pick.) Ants love this sugary fluid. They love it so much that they look after aphids to ensure a steady supply. That's right—they tend herds of aphids to milk them for their honeydew.

If tapping all that sap doesn't put a plant under the weather, aphids can cause problems in another way. Moving around to feed, they can spread viruses from an infected plant to a healthy one.

Aphids have unusual life cycles. They may swap between the standard method of reproduction—involving males and females producing eggs—to a type of cloning in which females give birth to daughters without male aphids playing any part (parthenogenesis). The process used depends on the time of year and the amount of food available. Even more peculiar, a female aphid may have daughters developing inside her, which in turn contain their own daughters. With this telescoping of generations it's no wonder that aphids can undergo population explosions.

Pal or pest? **Pest**

How do I deal with them?

White oil is effective but will kill other insects. Ladybirds, hoverflies and antlions all love aphids on the menu and will hoe into them if given the chance. Minute parasitoid wasps lay their eggs on aphids, which then provide fresh food for the growing wasp grubs. These wasps are available from commercial growers.

COCKROACHES

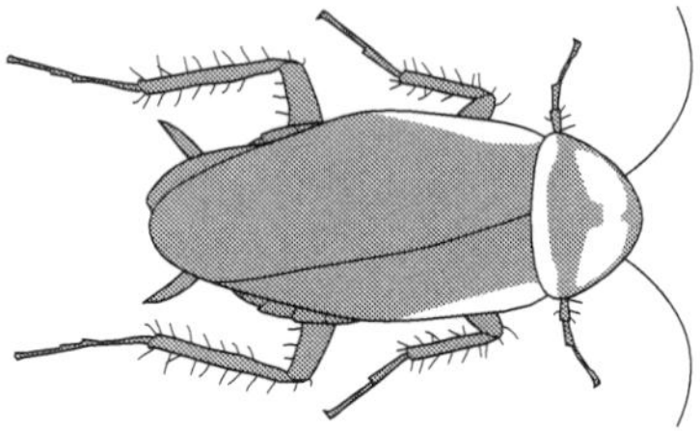

They're not all bad. Honestly. A few introduced species make their presence felt in the kitchen and bathroom and they *all* get a bad reputation. It's true that those introduced species are real pests but most native cockroaches are blameless.

Cockroaches all look much the same, so how do you tell them apart? Although they vary from fingernail-size to whoppers that would cover your palm, they are all oval-shaped with long whip-like antennae and a broad plate just behind the head. A pair of small pointed appendages (cerci) stick out from the back end. Depending on species and age, cockroaches may have two pairs of wings that lie flat against the back when not in use or may be wingless.

'Australian' and American cockroaches are whoppers—up to 5 cm long—and are a greasy, waxy brown with yellow markings on their backs. Adults have wings that overlap when the insects are crawling around. The native *Drymaplaneta* looks similar to the introduced pests but is wingless. The 'German' cockroach is smaller—only about 1.5 cm long. It ranges in colour from yellowish to almost black. Two dark stripes running along the body distinguish this from other household cockroaches.

Surinam cockroaches live in compost heaps. These black insects have bronze or brown wings and grow to about 2.5 cm.

Housebound cockroaches prefer warm, dark places, ranging from rubbish bins and the lagging around water heaters to kitchen cupboards. They eat everything so are capable of finding food anywhere. You might be glad to read that cockroaches do not necessarily indicate unsanitary conditions—although large infestations can make places unsanitary very quickly.

Cockroaches are neither fussy nor delicate diners. They eat leftovers, paper, poo and leather. They will even nibble dead skin from your toes, if you let them. (So I'm told.) Not only do cockroaches poo on everything, they also barf with abandon while eating. These unpleasant habits mean they can spread diseases. We know they can distribute viruses and bacteria and also parasitic worms.

Cockroach egg cases (oothecae) are brown and crimped at one end, and are often glued to skirting boards and even book spines. You often see female cockroaches with an egg case still attached to her rear end as she looks for somewhere to leave the next batch of bad-mannered invaders.

Pal or pest?
Introduced species are pests.

How do I deal with them?

Although cleanliness helps, a clean house is not necessarily a cockroach-free house. Keeping surfaces free of cockroach poo and vomit will minimise the chance of diseases. (And is also a generally good idea.)

Geckos will deal with the small cockroaches. Sticky traps are effective, but watch out for collateral damage—like trapping the geckos themselves. Cockroaches will come to baits (p. 214). In warmer parts of the country, that's an ongoing battle.

On the other hand, native cockroaches make interesting pets. The giant (8 cm) *Macropanesthia rhinoceros* is reared commercially for sale in Australia. It's slow-moving and flightless, and seems to be just about trouble-free.

EARWIGS

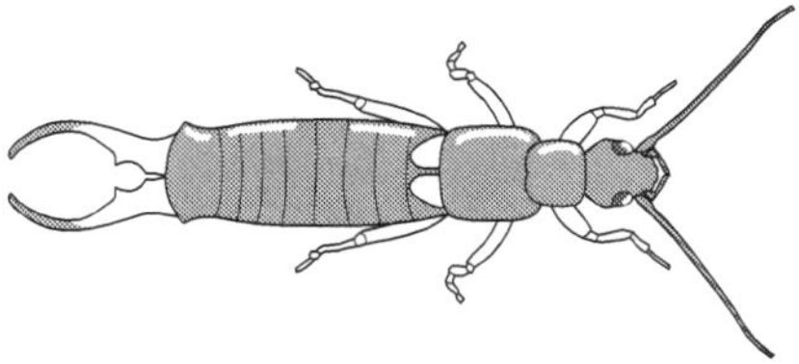

Lift up a regularly watered flower pot and you'll send an assortment of diminutive critters searching for cover. Some trundle, some dash and some scurry. Earwigs are scurriers. These long-bodied insects move quickly, exploring every gap for a place to hide. In the soil, that is. Despite the common name, earwigs aren't particularly fond of ears (or wigs).

Adult earwigs are easy to identify because they sport long pincers (cerci) at the rear end. In males, they are curved towards each other. Those of females are more or less straight. Females often use their cerci for domestic activities, such as carrying food and nesting material. Earwigs are among the few insects that not only build nests for their eggs but also take care of their young. If you disturb a nest, which is a small chamber in the soil, you may mistake the young earwigs for termites. They are similar in appearance but young 'uns usually have Mum in attendance. Female earwigs will even feed their family, a behaviour that's unusual among most non-social insects.

Although there are more than 60 species of native earwig, the introduced European species *Forficula auricularia* is the most likely resident in city and suburban gardens. It has a varied diet, eating everything from other insects to plants to fungi.

Pal or pest?
In large numbers, they can be pests when they feed on seedlings.

How do I deal with them?

Place wet newspapers in the garden to lure them to one spot. Collect the newspaper and deal with them as you see fit. You can relocate them to the compost heap or kill them by drowning in hot soapy water.

TERMITES

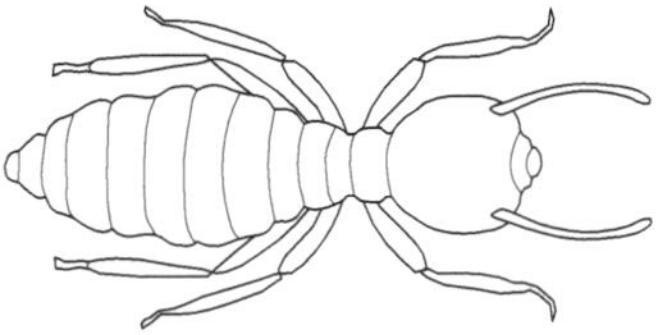

The floorboards seem to be okay. No cracks, no splits. Then you step on them and they crumble into sawdust and splinters. Termites have been at work, tunnelling into the dry wood and chewing away at it from the inside. Their interior demolition leaves the outside intact, so you won't realise what's been happening until your foot goes through the floor . . .

Termites look innocuous. Nothing in their appearance indicates that these small, pale insects are the scourge of home owners across the country. But these little insects have two characteristics that put them on the Most Not Wanted list—they eat plant material (including dead wood) and they live in colonies. That's a dangerous combination if you own a wood-framed house.

They are often called 'white ants', although they aren't related to true ants (p. 62). Like their namesakes, they construct nests, from where worker termites march out to gather food to share with the rest of the colony. Soldier termites, armed with strong jaws or a chemical spray, defend the nest from attackers. But despite their impressive armoury, termites are a favourite food for a wide range of native animals from velvet worms (p. 39) to echidnas (p. 139).

Pal or pest?
Wood-eating species are pests of living and dead timber. Fortunately, the majority of termite species are not home-eaters.

How do I deal with them?

Don't muck about with termites in the home. If building a new house or if your house is already infested, get professional advice.

CRICKETS

Mole cricket

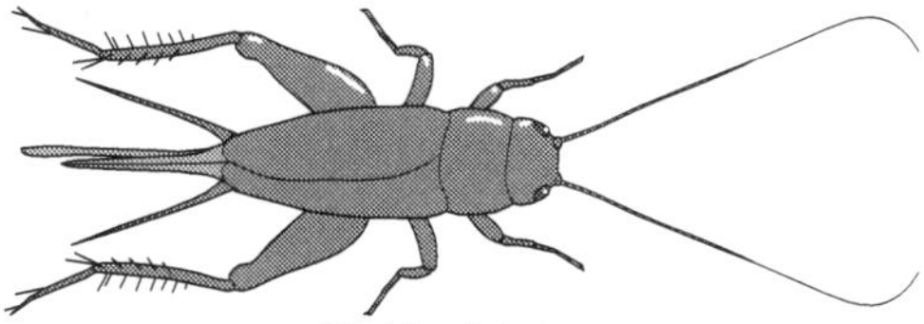

Field cricket

You are more likely to hear crickets than to see them. Males sing on warm, still nights to attract females. Their trilling calls are a sign that summer is on its way.

Field crickets are sturdy insects with long antennae and robust hind legs. Although they're reluctant to show themselves, you may encounter them at night while they're out searching for food. Field crickets feed on seedlings and decaying leaves but will also dine on dead insects, squashed snails and dog food. They're not finicky eaters and will chow down on whatever they find.

Mole crickets are strange-looking animals—long and bulky with an armour-plated head, a bloated body and big, clawed front legs that make them look as though they've been downing steroids by the bucketful. Mole crickets are expert diggers, as their common name suggests. They excavate burrows in lawns and other open areas, using those front legs as shovels and the claws on them to slice through plant roots. Once they've built a retreat, they sit in the entrance and belt out their low-pitched, almost frog-like *crick-crick-crick*. The chamber acts as a resonator, amplifying a loud call into an earsplitting one.

Pal or pest?

Cricket songs can drive people to distraction. Field crickets can be a pest in newly planted vegie gardens.

How do I deal with them?

Lots of animals love crickets, so biological control is the best long-term solution. Foam earplugs may reduce the intrusive calls. Dig up mole cricket burrows, if you can locate them, to persuade the owner to move on.

ANTLIONS

Those tiny depressions in the sand might look as though they've been made by dripping water but they don't follow the line of the eaves. If you watch for a while, you might see an ant wandering up to one of the little pits. It explores the slopes for food. But then something flicks sand grains at it and it tumbles to the bottom . . . where a pair of jaws snaps shut on the hapless insect.

You've got antlions. And you can guess how they got that name.

Antlions are young lacewings (p. 111). Strictly speaking, the term 'antlion' refers to just one group among the lacewings—the pit diggers—but the larvae of the other groups are equally ferocious if not quite as industrious. Young owlflies have enormous trap jaws that are as long as their bodies. They hunt through the leaf litter and on low shrubs for insects. On encountering lunch, those giant jaws snap shut. Green lacewing larvae festoon their bodies with leftovers from earlier dinners. The uneaten remains camouflage the predator without sending a warning signal to the next meal. Yes, it's a different world.

Pal or pest?
Antlions and other lacewings feed on aphids and other pest insects.

How do I deal with them?

Encourage them by providing areas of sand in which they can dig their pitfall traps. If you can persuade adults to stick around (p. 211), the young will soon appear.

BOOKLICE

Or barklice, depending on whether they're indoors or out. Booklice are tiny grey or black insects, with or without wings, that live among leaves, under bark and in stored products, including paper. They look a little like robust aphids (p. 74) in size and shape, but differ in that they hold their wings over their back like a pitched tent.

Outdoors, they feed on fungi, lichen and pollen. So what are they doing looking for food among your books? They're partial to the spots of mould (fungus), which often grow on paper under poorly ventilated conditions, and the glues used in book binding. When you're less than 2 mm long, there's a banquet on every bookshelf.

Pal or pest?
They can be a pest if they infest the pantry or library.

How do I deal with them?

It is difficult to keep them at bay. They prefer warm, humid conditions, so keeping larders, libraries and offices well ventilated. Infestations in pantries can be controlled by cleaning out all suitable hiding places (including drawer runners and the corners between shelves and walls) and drying them thoroughly before replacing the contents. Freezing dry goods for several days will kill eggs and adults to reduce the chance of re-infestation.

THRIPS

For most of the year, thrips go about their business unseen by all but keen gardeners (and thrips-studying entomologists).

Thrips are tiny black insects, either flightless or with two pairs of feathery wings. In summer, they often swarm in great numbers on flowers and fruit. That's when they make their presence known to the wider circle.

Thrips (the name applies to one or millions) feed on plant sap. They scrape away the surface layer and suck up the liquid that oozes from the damaged cells. Depending on the part of the plant to which those cells belong, the thrips' bad table manners may result in misshapen and distorted flowers or fruit. Because they hide in buds, their handiwork is sometimes the first clue that they're about. They may also transmit diseases between plants.

On the plus side, thrips act as pollinators when they travel from flower to flower. A few species are also predators of scale insects (p. 198).

Pal or pest?

In large numbers, sap-sucking thrips are pests.

How do I deal with them?

Healthy plants can usually compensate for the problems caused by thrips.

Biological control using predatory mites, other thrips, wasps and bugs will keep down numbers to give the plants a better than fighting chance. Sticky traps will catch some of the thrips population, so it might be worth using those to support the predators. Thrips have colour preferences—yellow and blue traps attract different species.

LICE AND NITS

Just writing about lice makes me want to scratch my head. Are you scratching as you read this?

Head lice are parasites. They feed on blood, which they draw from their human hosts. When they bite—each insect does this several times a day—lice inject saliva into the wound. This causes a persistent itch. When a bunch of lice take meals at different times, it's no surprise that the itching can drive someone to distraction.

Adult lice are small (2–4 mm) and greyish with six robust legs. Each leg ends in a curved claw that is used to drag the louse through forests of hair. A female louse can lay up to 300 eggs during her short life. She glues these eggs (nits) onto hair within 2 cm of the scalp. The glue is so strong that normal washing won't dislodge them. Close up, nits looks like tiny yellowish pepper pots, covered in pits or perforations.

The perforations allow air through, so the developing louse can breathe. When ready to hatch, the louse pumps itself up with air and pushes off the lid of the egg. From egg to hatching takes between 1 and 3 weeks, depending on the temperature and humidity.

Lice are really tied to their hosts. Adults die in less than a week if deprived of food. (That's your blood.) They also experience problems if the food source's skin temperature changes. Too cold (i.e. dead) and they're off. Too warm (above 40°C) and they can't feed.

Are you scratching now?

How do I deal with them?

Check for lice by examining the scalp under a strong light. Adult lice can move rapidly, so you might not spot them, but you should be able to see nits attached to hair. A more thorough method requires applying conditioner to clean, dry hair and combing it through with a fine tooth comb. After each sweep, wipe the comb on a tissue and look for lice or nits. Every section of hair should be combed four times or more.

You can also use the combing method to kill lice. To have a chance at clearing up the infestation, you'll have to comb thoroughly every other day for three or four weeks.

Pharmacies sell lotions, foams and shampoos that kill lice. After an initial application these should be applied a second time, seven to ten days later, to get the lice that might have hatched after the first application. Not all lice are susceptible to all products. If they are resistant, your pharmacist may be able to recommend an alternative solution.

Head lice move from person to person through contact. If one person in a household has them, everyone should get checked too. It takes a big effort to get rid of lice.

BEDBUGS

For a long time, bedbugs featured only in stories told by travellers who'd gone overseas and stayed in the worst dives. But now they're finding their way into tales of everyday tourists. Bedbugs are undergoing a resurgence.

Often detected first by their bites, they are bloodfeeders that live close to people. These oval-bodied bugs are about

4–9 mm long. They are an even brown colour before feeding, but afterwards they appear striped because the abdomen is expanded with its blood dinner. Apart from the bites and the insects themselves, clues to infestations include spots of poo near feeding sites, tiny pearly-white eggs and cast-off skins.

Females live for many months (sometimes years), during which time they lay hundreds of eggs. Unlike lice, they can endure starvation. They may live for more than a year without food. People show different reactions to bites, ranging from no response to bad irritation and disturbed sleep. Fortunately, bedbugs are not known to spread disease in Australia.

They live in bed linen, mattress seams and around bedheads, in bed frames, behind paintings and in bedroom furniture. Travellers can bring home an infestation in luggage or clothing. That's really sharing those holiday experiences!

Pal or pest?

How do I deal with them?

Wash bed linen, preferably at a high temperature. Vacuum repeatedly and thoroughly. Steam cleaning is also effective. If an item cannot be washed, freezing is an effective way of killing bugs.

Be careful about second-hand furniture (especially wardrobes and other bedroom furniture) because it may harbour bedbugs.

PRAYING MANTISES

There's something a little sinister about praying mantises. It's not only the way they stalk their dinner but also the manner in which they groom themselves. Mantises are very *fastidious* predators.

They're unmistakeable—long-bodied and long-legged, with a strange triangular head and big eyes. *All the better to see you with.* The front legs are adapted for seizing and holding prey. *All the better to catch you with.* And their jaws are so tough they can bite clean through the armour-plating of most insects. *All the better to eat you with.* Flies probably have nightmares about praying mantises.

They eat whatever they can grab with their front legs.

Folded neatly when not in use, the legs are held in front of the face in a way that resembles someone at prayer. (The scientific name of the European mantis is *Mantis religiosa*.) When a mantis spies a fly or other insect, the front legs straighten out and snatch dinner from its perch. Spines along the inner surface make sure that dinner doesn't get a second chance.

Females of the common garden mantis attach their egg cases (oothecae) to tree branches and fence posts. Newly hatched mantises often resemble long-legged ants in both appearance and behaviour, but a close look reveals that the front legs are not what you'd expect on an ant.

Pal or pest?
They eat pest insects.

How do I deal with them?

Be careful with pest-repellents in the garden because praying mantises are susceptible to poisons.

STICK INSECTS

Q: What's brown and sticky?
A: A stick insect. I'm surprised you had to ask.

Masters of disguise, stick insects are more common that you might think. Their long, thin bodies look so much like twigs that they blend almost perfectly with their surroundings. You rarely spot them where they're in their natural habitat. They are most often seen when they fly to lights at night and the camouflage is no longer effective. Those visitors are usually males—females of most species are wingless.

Several of the larger species are popular as pets both here and overseas. The giant prickly stick insect is one of the world's largest insects. Females are up to 20 cm long and covered with spines and spikes. Females of the even longer goliath stick insect reach up to 25 cm.

Breeding in stick insects is full of surprises. Females often produce young without any help from males. Eggs resemble plant seeds and are coated with a mixture of substances that ants love to eat. The ants carry the eggs back to their nests, where they remain until they hatch. The ants get a snack, the eggs are protected—everybody wins.

Stick insects feed exclusively on leaves, which seems only fair.

Pal or pest?
Some species can be pests if they occur in large numbers.

How do I deal with them?

Pest stick insects are best left to insect-eating birds. They've got better eyesight and are paying closer attention than you.

SILVERFISH

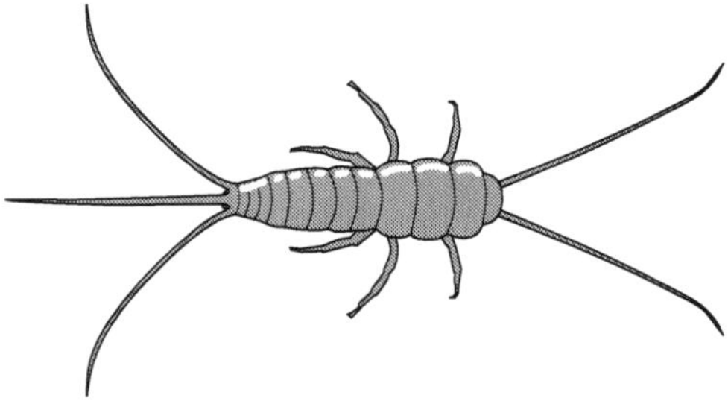

They're not fish but they are silver(y). The sheen on these little critters comes from the fine scales that brush off like dust when you pick them up. At first glance, they resemble small cockroaches (p. 76): wingless, with long antennae and pointed appendages (cerci) sticking out from the rear end. But a closer examination reveals the differences. Silverfish have tapered bodies clearly divided into segments and possess what looks like three thin tails.

Fast-moving and shy, they keep a low profile around the house. You might see them when you're spring-cleaning neglected corners, but they usually make their presence felt by their eating habits. Out in the garden, silverfish are ace recyclers, feeding on lichen and decaying plants and giving the soil a boost with their poo. But a few species prefer to live alongside us in our warm and cosy homes. These silverfish have a taste for glue, natural fabrics and dry food, none of which we want to share with them. Their surreptitious nibbling damages books, cloth and the contents of the kitchen cupboard.

Pal or pest?
Indoors, silverfish are pests.

How do I deal with them?

Vacuum regularly, especially in the corners. Clean out bookshelves and cardboard boxes used for storage and give them a spray with a pyrethrum-based insecticide. Eucalyptus oil may work as a repellent, so use it to wipe down drawers or shelves where silverfish may lurk.

SLATERS

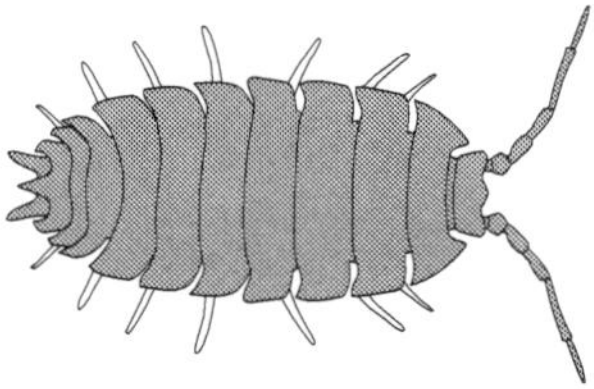

You can see the similarity between slaters and their landhopper cousins (p. 43). Slaters are flattened from top to bottom; landhoppers are flattened from side to side. And if you use a bit more imagination, you can see the link between both of these and their more distant relatives, the crayfish and lobster.

Slaters trundle about the garden looking for rotting fruit and vegetables, leaves and fungi. They are grey or brown segmented animals with elbowed antennae and multiple legs. When disturbed, they will either scuttle under cover or curl up. Some slaters can roll themselves into an armour-plated ball.

Although they can resist short-term dryness, they are strongly dependent on moisture. To avoid dehydration, slaters spend their days in damp soil and mulch or under stones and plant pots and move around only by night.

Several species have been accidentally introduced from Europe. The pill bug and the common slater are among those that keep us company in the garden.

Pal or pest?

Mostly pal. They eat decaying vegetable matter but may take an occasional nibble on seedlings. In high densities, those nibbles can grow into a problem.

How do I deal with them?

Rake over mulch to dry it out. Remove plant pots or raise them off the soil, so air can circulate beneath them, to reduce hiding places for slaters. They will also take snail baits (p. 214).

SNAILS AND SLUGS

On wet nights, snails and slugs come out in droves. Don't go outside in bare feet. The unexpected *crunch* is bad enough. What oozes between your toes is even worse.

Snails and slugs are the landlubber cousins of abalone, limpets, clams and squid. Although there's not much family resemblance on the outside, the similarity lies under the skin. One of the features shared by the slimy group is the way they tuck all the internal organs away in a thin-walled bag called the visceral mass. In snails, this is corkscrewed into the shell. In slugs (which are nothing more than shell-less snails), the visceral mass is packed into the rest of the body. This means they can squeeze into tiny spaces while snails stare in wonder.

Most of our garden snails and slugs have come into Australia from Europe. The common garden snail is widespread and abundant, especially in cooler areas. It sports a large (30–40 mm), round, brown and black mottled shell. During the day, you'll find them sealed onto walls and plant pots. At night and on rainy days, they slide around in search of seedlings and other vegetable matter. It is reported to have been introduced in the late 1800s as food . . . for blackbirds. Someone didn't think that move all the way through.

White snails are another European pest. They prefer drier areas and are often found in huge numbers stuck onto fence posts, tree trunks or low bushes by the beach. This climbing habit extends to cereal crops, so when the wheat is harvested, the snails come with it. One or two individuals don't cause problems but scale that up . . .

Not all introduced snails are nuisances. The glassy, flat garlic snail lives in garden mulch and eats other small Spineless and rotting vegetation.

Leopard slugs are spectacular—in a slimy, sluggy way. Coloured silver-grey with black spots and blotches, these giant slugs are unmistakeable. They have certainly earned the 'maximus' in their scientific names because adult slugs can grow up to 20 cm long.

Close behind those are the shorter (15 cm) but bulkier black slugs. They are jet black and produce the stickiest, ickiest, slimiest slime of all introduced slugs. If you have to pick them up, always use gloves.

Other common types of slugs are less impressive. Great yellow slugs are yellowish with khaki spots and blotches. Grey field slugs are pale pinky-grey to light brown, often with random dark grey markings. Striped field slugs are similar in colour but also have two dark stripes running back from the head.

Not all introduced slugs have a European origin. Gardens in warmer parts of the north and east may host a couple of species that look like large lumps of cookie dough after one round with the rolling pin. *Vaginulus plebeius* from Central America is plain brown, whereas *Laevicaulis alte* from tropical Asia is dark grey with a pale stripe running down its back.

Australia has a small variety of native slugs of which the red-triangle slug is best known. They come in shades of green, grey and white with a small red triangle on the back (pointing right). Even if you don't spot the animals, you may see the zigzag feeding trails they leave on smooth-barked trees. Common in gardens between Brisbane and Sydney, these slugs do no damage to vegie gardens or seedlings.

Pal or pest?
Many introduced species are pests.

How do I deal with them?

Collect snails and slugs by (gloved) hand and crush them or feed them to the ducks, bluetongues or stumpy-tails. (Do this only if the pests are guaranteed free of snail pellets.)

The odd thing about snails and slugs is they like to have a beer. A beer trap (p. 214) is an excellent way of reducing their numbers while not feeling too bad about their destruction. (You can tell yourself they've died happy.)

Snail baits work well. Those containing iron phosphates are less poisonous to people and pets than those with metaldehyde or methiocarb. Always place them in areas where children, pets and other animals can't get to them.

FLIERS

FLIES

Hoverfly

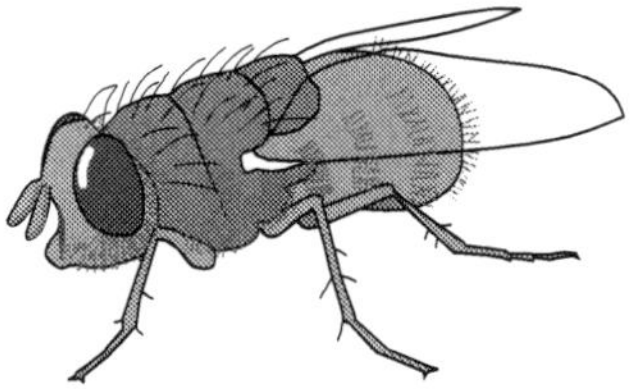

Blowfly

What's an Australian summer without the buzz of blowies and the occasional housefly up the nose? Despite our ill will towards them, flies of all shapes and sizes play an important part in making the world run smoothly.

How many shapes and sizes? The group includes minute midges about 1 mm long and massive robber flies with wingspans of up to 75 mm. There are flies with hammer heads and those that look as though they're walking on stilts. They come in all colours—metallic greens and blues, spots, stripes and a combination of both.

Blowflies, houseflies and fleshflies are always on the lookout for something putrid. Rotten food, poo, dead animals . . . they aren't fussy. Maggots—baby flies—live on our waste and do a great service in cleaning up the mess. Unfortunately, their parents have a hygiene problem, shifting between the dirty and clean and spreading germs on their grubby feet.

Not all flies have such bad manners. You may notice black and yellow striped insects hovering around flowers. They look like slim-line bees but are more elegant and precise in their flight. These are hoverflies, stingless insects that borrow protection from their resemblance to more dangerous species. Watch them for long enough and you'll get to know the difference in the way they fly. Bees are good but hoverflies are *amazing*.

Dumpy, slow-flying horse or March flies feed on blood. Attracted to dark colours, they can bite through thin fabric. (They'll have a go at denim but are usually unsuccessful.) When they bite, you'll know about it. Their mouthparts carve into the skin, slicing through tiny blood vessels. Like mosquitoes, female March flies require a blood meal before laying eggs. Males feed on nectar and pollen.

Strictly speaking, fruit flies are those small flies with coloured eyes and black-patterned wings that you often see sun-baking on leaves. If you watch them for long enough, you might catch them doing a little mating dance—males shuffle and wiggle their wings in a way that female flies find irresistible. The name is also used for the tiny flies that rise in swarms from the fruit bowl when you pick out the brown bananas.

Pal or pest?
Blowies, houseflies, March flies and fruit flies are pests. Hoverflies are pals.

How do I deal with them?

Insect screens on windows and doors stop blowies entering the house. Cover food to ensure they don't leave their mucky footprints all over it. Traps (p. 211) baited with a cube of rotten meat or bananas are effective, but use them judiciously or you may end up attracting even more flies. (If you don't fancy that, try using the tray or absorbent lining from packaged meat livened up with some diluted Vegemite.)

In the garden, dispose of damaged and fallen fruit to prevent the spread of fruit fly. Protect ripening fruit with net sleeves (which also work against birds and possums). Avoid using sprays unless you're at your limit—they'll kill off all the predators that would otherwise have a field day with your flies.

MOSQUITOES

These little buzzers are more often heard than seen. The high-pitched whine of their wings is enough to wake all but the soundest sleeper. And when they *are* seen, it is usually during or after a bite. Then the next view is of a bloody smear with spindly legs. That's your blood, of course. The mosquito was having a snack.

Only female mosquitoes feed on blood. On finding a suitable source, they saw into skin with sharp mouthparts that slide against each other. Then they search for a blood vessel. If they don't hit one straight away, they try again at a different angle. Mosquito saliva delays clotting so the insect can get a meal before the blood stops flowing. It also causes a local reaction that includes redness, swelling and an infuriating itch.

That's not all. Mosquitoes transmit diseases. In Australia, they carry dengue, Ross River and Barmah Forest viruses and Murray Valley encephalitis. (Malaria is not a problem here.) They also spread heartworm to dogs. The diseases enter mosquitoes when they feed on infected blood and are passed on when they have the next meal.

Mosquitoes are associated with water. They lay their eggs in still water or damp soil that is likely to be flooded. The eggs hatch quickly—usually within 48 hours. Larvae are aquatic but breathe air. You'll see them in bird baths and just about anything that contains stagnant water. After a few days, the wriggling larvae turn into comma-shaped pupae and then emerge from the water's surface as winged adults.

Don't confuse mosquitoes with harmless crane flies. They look similar—long bodies, skinny legs and filmy wings—but are different sizes. Mosquitoes are small but crane flies are huge in comparison (up to 75 mm wingspan).

Pal or pest? **Pest**

How do I deal with them?

Empty out birdbaths and the saucers under plant pots every few days to ensure they don't harbour wrigglers. Check gutters, dog bowls and anything else that may trap water. They'll even live in the cups of bromeliads and bird's nest ferns.

The most effective mosquito repellents are those containing DEET, a synthetic substance, but lemon-scented tea tree oil and citronella will also put the biters off their food. Repellents containing these plant extracts have to be reapplied more frequently than the longer-lasting DEET.

Mosquito nets are excellent for keeping the little buzzers away at night. Make sure that the net doesn't touch your skin because they can stick their mouthparts through the mesh.

If bitten, treat the site with a cold pack (not ice) to reduce swelling. Antihistamines may relieve the itching. Scratching only prolongs the irritation and may introduce infections.

SAND FLIES OR BITING MIDGES

In parts of the United States, they're called 'no see ums'. That pretty much says it all. You'll feel the bite but might never spot the culprit. Not because they've made a rapid getaway but because they're so small.

Sand flies are tiny black or grey insects with disproportionately big bites. The largest flies are no more than 4 mm long; most are only half that size. If you own a good magnifying glass, you'll see that they have long bodies and skinny legs and look a bit like miniature hunchbacked mosquitoes. Not the prettiest of insects.

Females take a blood meal before laying their eggs. Because the young are aquatic, sand flies tend to hang around damp areas. Adults don't move far away from their breeding sites so they are associated with swamps, riverbanks, estuaries and mangroves. They are most active at dawn and dusk on still days. If it's windy, they'll stay at home.

Sand fly bites are intensely itchy. The irritation may take a few hours to develop and often lasts for days. Sometimes the bites produce blisters.

Pal or pest?

How do I deal with them?

Keep sand flies out of the house with very fine fly screens. Ceiling fans will stir up the air enough to dissuade them from landing.

When out and about in sand fly country, cover up as much as possible. It seems to be the only way to stop them biting. If you're sensitive to bites, apply insect repellent to exposed skin to give yourself a fighting chance.

LACEWINGS

Lacewings are distinctive and delicate fliers. They often flutter to lights at night, where they mingle with the sorts of insects that will probably end up as lunch for their young ones. As adults, many species of lacewing feed on nectar but as larvae they are voracious carnivores (see antlions, p. 85).

The common name comes from their two pairs of filmy wings, which are usually tented over the body. One of the most abundant species of lacewing is vivid green with iridescent, gem-like eyes. They are well camouflaged among leaves so you'd be lucky to spot them in their natural habitat.

Other species within the group include owlflies, which rest with their wings hanging down, and mantis flies, which have grasping forelegs that resemble those of praying mantises.

Some species of lacewings lay stalked eggs that look like miniature helium balloons on strings. You'll see them on leaves and fence palings. They are often arranged in a U-shape. Other lacewings stick their eggs to branches or drop them on the soil.

Because they are useful predators, several species are bred commercially for controlling aphids, white fly and small moths in vegetable and fruit crops.

Pal or pest?

How do I deal with them?

Lacewings, like most other insects, are vulnerable to pest sprays, so avoid using them if you want to encourage these predators to live in your garden.

BUTTERFLIES AND MOTHS

Australia is home to thousands of species of butterflies and moths. There's no clear-cut division between the two groups but, generally, butterflies are active by day, have thread-like antennae with little bumps at the end and sit with their wings held upright. Everything else is a moth. It's not foolproof but it's a handy rule of thumb.

As adults, all butterflies and most moths visit flowers to drink nectar. In their travels, they carry pollen from plant to plant, which is good news for fruit and vegie gardens. Their caterpillars (p. 26) aren't so helpful. Feeding on leaves, fruit or wood, depending on the species, they can wreak havoc if occurring in large numbers.

The small orange and brown skippers are common in gardens across the country. They rest with their front wings held upright and their hind wings flat. (There goes the rule of thumb!)

Many of the tiny blue butterflies that flit among grass stems lay their eggs near ant nests. The ants protect the caterpillars from predators, while the caterpillars feed the ants with sweet honeydew released from a gland near the end of the body.

White butterflies are among the first to take flight in spring. Introduced cabbage whites lay their eggs on cabbages and cauliflowers, making them the scourge of market gardeners. Native caper whites, with their black trimmed wings with checkerboard undersides, migrate in large numbers in search of food plants for the next generation.

The largest butterflies are birdwings. The orchard butterfly is a hefty black insect with red and white markings. Other birdwings are more colourful—both the Ulysses and blue triangle are black and vivid blue and the Cairns birdwing is black, emerald green and lemon yellow.

Wanderer or monarch butterflies are a striking combination of orange and black with white spots on the body. The bright colours warn would-be attackers that they're loaded with poisons.

The very abundant crow or oleander butterfly is dark with white spots. (The chrysalis of this species is extraordinary—it is silvered like a mirror.)

The Australian admiral and painted lady are lively shades of orange, yellow and black. They are strong fliers and frequent visitors to gardens.

Most species of moths are not as well known as butterflies but a few do have high profiles.

Giant wood moths live up to their name. They are the size of small birds, fluttering about gum forests on wings more than 20 cm from tip to tip. Although adults don't feed, the caterpillars (also known as witchetty grubs) chew their way through trees.

Emperor gum moths have feathery antennae, woolly legs and body and orange, black and white bullseyes on their hind wings. Like the giant wood moths, they spend their entire adult period not eating.

Fruit-piercing moths suck juice from ripe fruit, causing havoc in orchards of all sizes. Their mouthparts are tough enough to break through the skin of citrus. They also like mangoes, lychees and guavas. These troublemakers have dull-coloured front wings and dramatic orange and black hind wings.

Bogong moths may not be so flashy but make their presence felt in another way. This species is known for its mass migrations from wintering spots in the lowlands to spring haunts in the mountains. During the trips there and back, they gather around lights in vast numbers. Just after the new Parliament House was opened in Canberra, the moths swarmed over it, prompting a swift redesign of outside lighting and airconditioning vents.

Pal or pest

Mostly pals as adults, although fruit-sucking moths are pests.

How do I deal with them?

Encourage adults to visit by planting nectar-rich flowers. Mix species that blossom at different times, so there is always a little something for them. Bees and honeyeaters will thank you too. If you want to persuade them to stay in your garden, you'll have to provide food plants for the caterpillars. Not one or two saplings, which they'll strip in a day, but a good supply to keep them going for several weeks.

Catch pests using pheromone traps (which target specific moths) or light traps (which attract everything). Reduce damage from fruit-sucking moths by bagging developing fruit. Corrugated cardboard wrapped around tree trunks provides a daytime hiding place from which you can pick off the moths at your leisure. Other animals will take advantage of this, so be careful as you detach it from the tree.

Many animals feed on moths, so you might choose to let them do their thing. Speed up this process by introducing parasitoid wasps that attack eggs.

BEES

Have you ever looked at a bee's knees? Take a peek at honey bees when they're visiting flowers and you'll see that their back legs carry bags of yellow pollen. They pick it up from blossoms, pack it in to bundles and stick it to their knees.

It's a handy way of lugging around a load of food to take back to the nest.

Not all bees are quite so tidy. Even fastidious honey bees miss the odd spot of pollen here and there. And these occasional oversights make these insects so important—they transfer pollen to other flowers and thus ensure the next generation of plants.

Australia has hundreds of different types of bees. Many of them are small and black or have a metallic sheen. They don't look much like the furry, orange and black honey bees and are easy to overlook or mistake for flies. Next time you see a little winged insect roving across a daisy flower, check it out—it's probably a native bee collecting pollen for its young.

Of course, quite a few species are big and fuzzy. Leaf-cutter bees have grey stripes and red or orange caps and tails. They snip neat circles out of leaves to make the walls of their nests.

Blue-banded bees are striped in black and electric blue. Females dig tunnels in sand and soft stone, while the males snooze at night clamped onto twigs by their jaws. Males of the rotund, orange-furred teddy bear bees share this unusual habit.

Cuckoo bees, unmistakeable with their sky-blue polka dots or neon blue splodges, lay their eggs in the nests of other species.

Reed bees live in hollow stems of lantana and tree fern fronds. Carpenter bees excavate burrows in banksia or paperbarks. They are very fond of the flower stalks of grass trees.

Most native bees are not big honey producers. Stingless bees are the exception. In the wild, they nest together in colonies and make 'sugarbag', a fine wild honey. These bees are available commercially for home production but are nowhere near as prolific as honey bees.

Although bees are not usually aggressive, most bees will sting in self-defence. Only stingless bees are unable to do this (as the name suggests).

Pal or pest?
Pal—mostly. Feral honey bees can be pests.

How do I deal with them?

Encourage native bees by planting flowers rich in pollen and nectar. Give native bees a helping hand by providing specially designed accommodation made from old hardwood blocks with burrows drilled in them. They will also appreciate bundles of bamboo slung from horizontal tree branches.

Honey bees can be a nuisance if they swarm in your garden. If this happens, call your local beekeeping group or a professional pest controller. Report any sightings of introduced bumble bees on the mainland to your state Department of Primary Industries (p. 237).

If stung by a bee, watch for any signs of a reaction (p. 221). If you have a known bee allergy, seek medical attention immediately.

WASPS

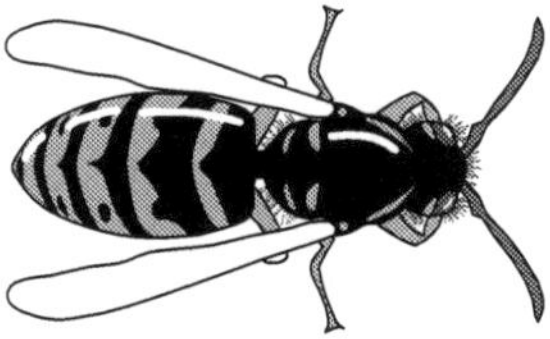

Wasp-waisted but not always waspish, these sleek cousins of bees and ants have lifestyles that are sometimes really bizarre.

The highest profile wasps are probably the black and yellow introduced European and English wasps. They build their papier-mâché nests in trees, under eaves or in soil and sally forth from them to raid barbecues and picnics. In urban areas, fences and weatherboards provide a source of material for the nests. You'll often see wasps stripping off slivers of wood, which they chew into a pulp and glue into a home for their family. When not tucking into your lunch, wasps eat a range of food including insects and fruit.

Paper wasps are similar in appearance to European wasps. They often build their nests in just the wrong location—on a verandah, under the eaves or on a clothes-line.

Many of our native wasps are solitary. Females lay their eggs on—or in—a caterpillar or other insect, which then provides food for the growing wasp larva. (The life cycle in *Alien* appears to have been based on one of these wasps.)

In spring and summer, brightly coloured flower wasps visit blossoming plants to drink nectar. These species are important pollinators. The black flower wasp is jet black with a metallic blue sheen. You'll often see these insects flying low over the ground. When they land, they will burrow into the soil to look for curl grubs, which are the hosts for the wasps' larvae.

Despite their common names, blue ants and velvet ants are also wasps. Only males have wings; females are flightless and look very much like ants. They lay their eggs on mole crickets, which they track down in their burrows, or on the young of other wasps.

Mud daubers build mud nests in caves, on cliffs and around sheds and houses. They lay a single egg in each nest, which they stock up with paralysed spiders and insects as fresh food for the growing offspring.

Tiny wasps that lay their eggs on or in pest insects are bred on farms for biological control. They are often very fussy about just where they leave their young, so they target particular species.

Pal or pest?

Most native species are pals.
European and English wasps are pests.
Paper wasps can be pests in the wrong place.

How do I deal with them?

Destroying nests is the only successful way of getting rid of introduced wasps. Because nests can contain 2000 or more individuals, each with a sting than can be used multiple times, it's best to get professionals in to remove the nest. Your local council may be able to offer advice about this.

Wasp stings can be dangerous if you have an allergic reaction, have been stung on the throat or mouth or have been stung multiple times in a single incident (p. 221).

Parasitoids are raised on a commercial scale to keep down pests in crops. Consider using them if you have serious problems in your garden.

DRAGONFLIES

Dragonflies have collected a number of nicknames, none of them affectionate. Horse stinger, ear cutter and Devil's darning needle among others. Next to those, 'dragonfly' seems like a warm and friendly epithet. For the record, they don't sting, are not known to snip ears and can't be threaded with darning wool.

Adult dragonflies have two pairs of transparent wings and long, thin bodies, which are often vividly coloured in red or blue. They have huge eyes that give them excellent sight. They use it to hunt other insects, which they catch in flight.

Larvae (nymphs) live in fresh water, where they crawl across the mud in search of prey. Small ones feed on mosquito wrigglers and blood worms. Larger ones eat whatever they can overpower, including tadpoles and small fish. When not feeding, their extendable mouthparts (the mask) are folded away under the head. As soon as something edible comes within striking range, the mask shoots out and clamps down on dinner.

That isn't the only odd thing about dragonfly nymphs. Like fish, they have gills for breathing underwater. But quite unlike fish, their gills stick out from their backsides. Let's all be grateful that no-one's come up with a nickname based on that feature.

Pal or pest?

How do I deal with them?

Encourage dragonflies by building a pond with suitable perches at the water's edge. Once established they will feed on pests on land and in the water.

THE OTHER 5 PER CENT: NOT THE SPINELESS

TADPOLES

Frogs and toads are animals of two worlds. As youngsters, they live in water as tadpoles, breathing through gills and swimming with the aid of a long tail. When they become adults, they undergo a transformation (metamorphosis) and turn into four-legged, air-breathing land dwellers.

Frogs and toads start life wrapped in a squidgy egg case, which keeps the growing tadpole safe from predators and parasites. But the case is not waterproof, so it has to be kept moist to stop it drying out. To make sure the eggs don't dehydrate, most frogs lay them in water. Others put them somewhere that is always damp—in burrows or leaf litter. Frogs usually lay their eggs in masses, but cane toads produce them in long strings that tangle in water weeds.

As the tadpole develops inside its jelly coat, it gets all its food from a blob of yolk. Once it breaks out, it feeds on algae in the water. At first, tadpoles look more like fish than they do adult frogs. But after days or weeks (depending on the species), the taddies begin their transformation. First, their hind legs grow from little buds on either side of the tail. Then the front legs develop. Finally, the tail is reabsorbed and the tadpole takes on definite frogginess. It's time to make the move onto land.

Pal or pest?
Frog tadpoles are pals. Cane toad tadpoles are pests.

How do I deal with them?

Remove cane toad eggs from the water and allow them to dehydrate.

FROGS

What Australia lacks in range of amphibians—no native toads, no salamanders, newts or caecilians—we make up for in sheer froggy diversity. We've got frogs everywhere. They're even found in the middle of the desert, buried deep in the sand.

Different regions have their characteristic species. Around Perth and the southwest, motorbike frogs and slender tree frogs visit gardens. Motorbike frogs are large, brown to green frogs with a crazy call—they sound like a motorbike changing gear and revving. Slender tree frogs are more restrained. They communicate with a sharp *peep*.

In North Queensland, it pays to check out the toilet bowl before you sit down. You might spot a green foot sticking out from under the rim. Green tree frogs like to tuck themselves away in the most unexpected places. They often sit in downpipes and drains, where they can make the most of their calls. Other tropical frogs are not so comfortable inside the house but are happy to hang around in the garden and on verandahs. The dainty green tree frog is a stunning leaf-green and yellow animal with a harsh, drawn-out call. The slender green tree frog sounds like a cicada practising its song.

The common eastern froglet lives in any standing water from lagoons to ditches. They vary in colour from pale to dark brown with or without stripes and blotches. Their repeated two-syllable *crick-et* is well known across most of southeastern Australia.

Different species of banjo frogs or pobblebonks occur all over the continent. The striped marsh frog is common in east coast gardens. This well-camouflaged black and brown animal spends the day under logs and among leaves, moving into water at night to call to mates. The song is a single *cluck*, similar to the sound you can make with your tongue against the roof of your mouth.

Even Central Australia is not frog-free. Several species spend the dry periods buried in sand and clay, emerging only after rain. They can spend months—maybe years—waiting patiently for the next storm. But the tiny, brown desert tree frog is out and about wherever there's some moisture.

Pal or pest?

Pal, although, when they're all calling at night, they can be pest-level noisy.

How do I deal with them?

Encourage frogs into your garden by providing a pond with plenty of plants in and around the water. If you build a pond with steep outer walls or surround it with a smooth barrier, cane toads won't be able to take advantage of it. Don't forget that frogs are great insect eaters, so be careful with the bug sprays. If you want to discourage frogs, either fill in the pond or add fish, dragonfly larvae and water bugs.

CANE TOADS

Large cane toads are unmistakeable. For a start, adults are huge—up to 20 cm long. Mix that with warty, dry-looking skin and a staccato call that's equal parts machine-gun and purr and you've got a toad. Small individuals are sometimes mixed up with burrowing frogs and other slow movers. Check for the presence of parotid glands, those large lumpy poison sacs behind the eyes. Although many frogs have them, they are really obvious in toads.

Cane toads are poisonous at all stages of their lives—eggs, tadpoles and adults. Only a few native species can deal with the poison. Some, like the keelback snake, are resistant to it. Others eat around the dangerous parts rather like humans dining on fugu (puffer fish).

Pal or pest?

How do I deal with them?

Prevent them taking advantage of frog ponds by building a toad-proof fence. Nothing helps toads more than a giving them a place to breed.

Direct action isn't pretty. You can remove toad eggs from ponds to prevent tadpoles hatching. This is one of the more effective methods of toad control.

Collect toads at night or on overcast days when they're on the move. The RSPCA has suggestions of humane ways to kill toads. It is important to dispose of toads and their eggs in a manner that keeps them away from other animals.

Always wear gloves when handling toads and take care not to disturb them too much because they can spray their poison a short distance. It's not something you want to get into your mouth or eyes.

GECKOS

You're just dozing off and something calls *chuck-chuck-chuck* from behind the curtain. A small lizard scuttles up the wall. It has big round eyes and toes with flattened tips. Congratulations. You've got geckos.

The chatty species is the introduced house gecko from Southeast Asia. Natives are usually silent, the only noise coming from the pattering of feet or rustling of an insect's wings as it disappears into a gecko's gullet.

They're little oddballs. Instead of eyelids, transparent scales cover and protect their eyes. Geckos use their tongues like windscreen wipers to keep them clean. They also drop their tails when threatened. The tail breaks at a weak spot close to its base. Blood vessels seal off automatically, stopping the gecko from bleeding to death. The tail writhes around while the rest of the gecko makes its getaway.

These lizards occur almost everywhere in Australia, although they are frequent house guests only in the north. Even urban gardens in Melbourne have their geckos. (Sorry, not Tasmania.) The marbled gecko is an unassuming little lizard. In the bush, it lives in logs and under tree bark. Fences and wood piles are the city equivalents.

Pal or pest?

Geckos clean up pest insects.
Surely you're not going to let the odd gecko poo put them into the pest category?

How do I deal with them?

Tight-fitting fly screens slow them down, but a few enterprising house geckos will always make it inside. You can improve the gecko-friendliness of a garden by building small rock piles or leaving fallen timber.

DRAGONS

They don't breathe fire or fly on long, webbed wings like their mythical namesakes, but dragons are impressive animals on their own small scale. You'll see them soaking up the sun on fences and rocks. When they spot other dragons, they signal to each other with head bobs and lazy waves. What look like friendly gestures are often warning signs. *This is my place. Keep moving.*

A few species are common garden visitors.

Jacky lizards occur from Adelaide to the Rockhampton area.

Water dragons live near waterways along the east coast. They are large, handsome dragons with spines on the top of the head and onto the neck. In summer, the males develop bright colours on their throats and chests and tiger stripes across the back and tail.

Bearded dragons are sandy-coloured lizards with rough scales on the throat. When disturbed, a dragon raises its head and extends its throat to present rows of sharp spines to an enemy. The effect is enough to make all but the bravest back off.

Frilled lizards are probably the most recognisable of the dragons. They have big collars that normally lie flat against their necks but can be spread out to make the lizards look bigger.

Pal or pest?

How do I deal with them?

Keep an eye on dogs and cats, which would otherwise tangle with dragons. Avoid using insect sprays in the garden, if possible, and let the dragons take care of the pests.

SKINKS

There are more types of skinks in Australia than any other type of lizard. They range from the bluetongues to the almost snake-like burrowing skinks, which are often dug up from the lawn or compost heap. Like dragons, skinks are big signallers and communicate with a range of tail wags and waves.

The smaller ones are difficult to identify, but some of the bigger species are familiar.

Bluetongues are plump, slow-moving lizards. These and stumpy-tails often sun themselves on roads, where they fall victim to cars. They eat insects, are especially fond of snails and will also eat fruit and flowers. To put it in a nutshell, they'll eat just about anything, really. When given a hard time, a bluetongue will open its mouth to show its bright blue tongue, inflate its body and hiss ferociously. And if all else fails, they'll bite. Hard.

Stumpy-tails or shinglebacks look like articulated pine cones. They have remarkably stable home lives . . . for lizards. Although males and females spend most of the year apart, each meets up with its partner at a regular rendezvous during the breeding season. They stay together for a couple of months, then separate.

Pal or pest?
Just keep bluetongues away from your strawberries.

How do I deal with them?

Don't use pesticides or snail bait. Keep pets away from skinks, which won't be able to protect themselves from cat or dog attack. If the bluetongues are too fond of your vegie patch put up a low barrier to keep them out.

SNAKES

Snakes attract myths like magnets attract iron filings. They do not wait until night to die. They are completely indifferent to milk. And there are no such things as hoop snakes (although it'd be cool if there were).

The truth about snakes is much weirder. They are deaf but can detect vibrations through their jaws . . . jaws that dislocate so they can swallow large prey. And while they do this, dragging their food in by moving each side of the jaw independently, they project a breathing tube from their mouths so they don't suffocate. That makes the milk-drinking myth look lame.

Australia has many different types of snakes. Of those, only a few are dangerous to people. But several of those dangerous ones are likely to visit suburban gardens.

Tiger snakes occur over southern Australia, including Tasmania. They are solid animals, often with dark bands (hence the name). In some areas, they may be only one colour, usually black. When threatened, tiger snakes flatten out the neck and raise their bodies off the ground.

Most snakes will clear off when they know you're on your way. They don't want to tangle with something as big as a human. But there are always exceptions. Death adders stay where they are and wait for food to come to them. The tip of a death adder's tail is thin, and the snake wiggles it like a worm to attract mice. When a mouse pounces on the worm, thinking how lucky it is, it doesn't take long before it realises that it wasn't so lucky after all. The death adder's reluctance to shift means that you might tread on one as it's loafing in the sun. This is where boots and long pants come in handy.

Brown snakes and taipans are common in grasslands and open areas. Both are very active snakes, hunting for mice and other warm-blooded animals. Despite the name, king brown snakes are actually closely related to red-bellied black snakes.

Harmless snakes also wander into gardens. In warmer areas, pythons are common visitors. Perhaps the best known are diamond or carpet pythons, but several other species may make an appearance. Although they are not venomous, pythons will bite if disturbed. They have numerous knife-sharp teeth that slice easily through skin. And just think where those teeth have been . . . (Hmmm. Perhaps 'non-venomous' would have been a better choice of word than 'harmless'.)

Green tree snakes put on a great show when disturbed. They arch and strike, but it's all bluff. Still, it's worth giving them some space to move away.

Brown tree snakes belong to a third category of snakes—those that are not exactly harmless but whose venom has a minor effect on people. Other common species in this group include whip snakes and the humbug-like bandy bandy.

Pal or pest?

Most snakes are pals because they keep down mice and other problem animals. But snakes in the wrong place are definitely pests.

How do I deal with them?

Discourage snakes from hanging around by clearing away anything that might act as a hiding place, especially close to the house. Keep lawns well trimmed.

If a snake has taken up residence in your garden and you'd prefer it to be somewhere else, call a professional snake catcher. Do not attempt to move it on. Do not try to catch it. In both cases, you'll put yourself at risk of a bite.

When you go into areas where snakes hang out, always wear boots and long pants. Sandals and shorts are not a good idea. Don't stick your hands or feet anywhere that you haven't checked out first. (That includes your shoes.)

If you have to lift anything, be careful. Roll logs towards you, so that anything underneath moves away from you. Lift debris in the same way.

In warmer weather, snakes may be out and about at night. Reduce the risk of accidentally stepping on one by carrying a torch. Heavy tread encourages them to move on, if they have enough room to escape.

If a snake does come into your house, block all doors to other parts of the house and leave open only the door leading outside. Often the snake will depart under its own steam. If this doesn't work, you will probably have to call in a professional snake catcher. If snakes are a problem in your location, have the snake catcher's phone number stuck on the refrigerator. It saves time.

For advice on first aid for snake bite, see p. 225.

ANTECHINUS

They may look like overgrown house mice but antechinuses are the miniature cousins of the Tasmanian devil. And they've got an attitude to match.

The yellow-footed antechinus of eastern and far southwestern Australia has a grey back and orange legs and feet. The tail, which is almost as long as the body, is tipped in black. This species often adopts suburban gardens as its territory. Some go further and regard the house as their territory too. Moths, cockroaches and spiders will disappear overnight, but they'll be replaced by a lot of antechinus poo. It's a fair trade. They will even steal food if they find something to their liking, but that is a rare occurrence.

Their natural diet includes insects, lizards, small birds and mice. As they feed, they turn their dinner's skin inside out. It's gruesome—but intriguing—evidence of your miniature marsupial visitors.

Pal or pest?

How do I deal with them?

Keep them out of the house by blocking access points. If you keep finches or other small birds, you may have to use another layer of fine wire mesh over the aviary because antechinus are good at squeezing through small gaps.

ECHIDNAS

Nothing else looks like an echidna except, perhaps, a very large toilet brush. Echidnas lumber around, nose to the ground, on the lookout for ants and termites. If disturbed, they will either pick up the pace or hunker down with head and feet tucked under. A covering of sharp spines keeps the world at bay. Don't try to pick them up or you'll regret it.

Echidnas have strong feet for digging and a long thin 'beak' with an even longer tongue used to extract lunch from underground nests. Those prickly spines are modified hair.

Although they are close relatives of the platypus, the family resemblance isn't immediately obvious. They both lay eggs, which no other mammals do. An echidna mum tucks the egg into a pouch on her tummy, keeping it warm and safe for the ten days until it hatches. The baby echidna (puggle) drinks milk secreted from a patch of skin on Mum's underside.

They are such odd animals that it's no surprise they even have remarkable fleas! At 4 mm long, the echidna flea is the biggest in the world.

Pal or pest?
Surely you're willing to forgive the odd bit of digging to have one of these around the place?

How do I deal with them?

Protect echidnas from dog attack. An encounter will end badly for both parties.

Don't pick them up. The spines are sharp, and echidnas are strong. Males also have poison-injecting spurs on the hind legs. If you have to transport an injured echidna, place it in a sack or wrap it in a blanket.

BANDICOOTS

With those long noses, you might mistake them for giant rats. But they've got short, unratty tails. Because they dig in the garden and move in stops and starts, you might think they're rabbits. But their ears are definitely unbunny-like. Given the digging evidence, it looks as though you've got bandicoots in your backyard.

Northern brown bandicoots and long-nosed bandicoots are garden residents in eastern Australia. They snuffle around in search of insects and other Spineless but won't turn up their (pointy) noses at mushrooms and tubers. They will excavate the lawn in search of curl grubs. A night's work might leave several conical pits in the middle of the turf along with a collection of cylindrical poos.

Pal or pest?
Pal because they eat curl grubs.
Pest if you're proud of your lawn (or have to look after a bowling green).

How do I deal with them?

Plant thickets of low, dense native vegetation to give bandicoots somewhere to hide during the day. Watch cats and dogs to make sure they don't frighten or attack your visitors.

Fence off vegie patches and other sensitive parts of the garden. As with rabbits, you will have to bury the wire *at least* 30 cm under the surface to stop them digging their way under it.

POSSUMS

Is there someone tap dancing on your roof in steel-toed boots? It *could* be an agile burglar but it's more likely to be a possum—either a brushtail or a ringtail, depending on your location.

While other marsupials have suffered from our activities, these two species are doing well. Not all over the country, it's true; but if you've seen them raiding rubbish bins, gorging on fruit or beheading roses, then you may have difficulty believing that they're not doing the same everywhere.

If you live on a bush block, you may also be visited by smaller (and better-mannered) sugar and squirrel gliders.

Pal or pest?
Pal at a distance. Pest close up.

How do I deal with them?

Do not feed them. No matter how cute and winsome they are. No matter how harmless they look. Do not feed the possums. It's not good for them and it's not good for you.

If you have a possum in your roof space, the best solution is to block off access points. If there are several potential points, try wadding up newspaper and jamming it into the holes during the day while the possum is snoozing. Don't do it so tightly that the poor thing can't escape. But when it pushes its way through, you'll know where it's getting in. While it's out and about, block up the hole with chicken wire.

Professional relocation is an option, although another possum may move in soon. Furthermore, the relocated possum may not survive when it's dropped off in another possum's territory. You can't relocate possums without a permit from your local Wildlife Service, so don't try it yourself or you'll end up with a fine as well as a possum problem.

MICE AND RATS

If there's a mouse loose about the house, chances are it's not native. Introduced mice and rats are strongly associated with people and tend to hang around inside where it's warm and the living is easy.

The house mouse is the only small rodent that commonly spends time indoors. (But see the entry on Antechinus, p. 137.) It is an expert filcher, stealing food and leaving little droppings in its place.

Black rats (which are brown, by the way) are the wild version of the pet rat. They climb well and are often seen running along fences and across roofs. Brown rats, which spend most of their lives on or under the ground, have an unpleasant reputation for aggression in the wild, but the domesticated form makes a docile and friendly pet.

A few common garden-dwelling rodents are native. Sleek-furred water rats live near rivers and swamps, often in the bustle of cities. In tropical Queensland, tree-climbing white-tailed rats will investigate kitchens. They can (and do) bite through tins.

Pal or pest?

Introduced species are pests. As are native species if they're inside the house.

How do I deal with them?

Block up access points around the house. If you're not sure how they're getting in, sprinkle flour in likely areas. You'll see their little paw prints and tail marks. Because they chew through just about everything, seal the gaps with steel wool. Clove or eucalyptus oil may also deter them.

If you live in white-tailed rat country make sure you don't leave windows or doors open at night. That applies to all areas with inquisitive rats—but white-tailed rats are in a class of their own.

RABBITS

Early settlers brought them in as dinner and they colonised Tasmania. Then Thomas Austin looked out across the plains southwest of Melbourne and decided that rabbits would liven up the place. Within 50 years, they'd taken over most of Australia and chewed their way through pastures and native vegetation, causing agricultural losses and extensive erosion. In a desperate attempt to stop the spread, the Western Australian government built not one, not two, but *three* rabbit-proof fences. They didn't work.

Such was the impact of rabbits that attempts were made to control them using diseases, the only way to keep them in check on a countrywide scale. At first, myxoma virus, which causes myxomatosis, had a serious impact on rabbit populations. But they soon bounced back. More recently, calicivirus is taking its toll.

Apart from raiding your garden—as if that's not bad enough—rabbits will also dig it up and cover it in droppings. They might look cute but they are inconsiderate visitors.

Pal or pest?

How do I deal with them?

Make your own rabbit-proof fences using fine-meshed wire. Ensure that the lower edge is buried deep in the soil or the bunnies will just dig under it. As long as there are no gaps, you'll have more success than the Western Australian government.

KANGAROOS AND WALLABIES

Despite being given a hard time over the years, a few of these icons of the bush have adapted to living close to us. At Anglesea Golf Course in Victoria, eastern grey kangaroos have done so well that they are a hazard on the fairways. They can't resist the lush greens.

Wallabies and their smaller cousins, bettongs and pademelons, leave the shelter of trees in the late afternoon to feed in outer suburban gardens. They feed on grass but will also nibble at flowers and shrubs and explore the vegie patch. If something takes their fancy, they'll push down fences to get to it. Skippy and his kin are very determined marsupials.

Pal or pest?
If they get into the vegie patch.

How do I deal with them?

Fence off areas to exclude 'roos and wallabies. The trick is to make a barrier that they cannot jump over, crawl under, push down or lean over (p. 208). Given that some of them are big and most of them are strong, this can be a challenge.

Don't feed them. Apart from giving them digestive problems, handouts may cause changes in behaviour. Kangaroos and wallabies have been known to become aggressive in locations where they are used to human contact. Remember that they are not only wild animals but also wild animals with big claws and a powerful kick. Someone is going to come out of a confrontation worse for wear and it probably won't be the 'roo.

CATS

They are great pets around the house but, after a few generations in the wild, domestic cats tend to turn into tabby thugs. Even lazy old Fluffy will take his chances in the garden when the right prey wanders into range. Feral cats will tackle anything up to the size of a common brushtail possum. Smaller animals are toast.

Pal or pest?
If not cared for responsibly, domestic cats can be a serious pest.

How do I deal with it?

It's difficult to keep cats confined. They're skilled climbers and leapers and can squeeze through tight gaps. Cat runs—like well-appointed aviaries *minus* the birds, of course—allow pets to enjoy the sun and fresh air while separating them from vulnerable wildlife. Locking cats in at night also reduces their impact on native fauna.

Protect nesting birds by wrapping plastic or metal guards around tree trunks. This stops cats from getting a grip on the bark, so they can't climb. (This works for possums too.)

Dense, spiky vegetation provides cover for small animals while deterring cats. Some of the densest and spikiest native plants also have the most beautiful flowers as a bonus.

Cat bells look cute but they aren't effective at warning wildlife. Most cats are quick learners and soon find a way to hunt without tinkling (as it were). They are also good at getting themselves out of belled collars.

FOXES

In the mid-1800s some bright sparks decided that what Australia really needed was a decent fox hunt, just like the ones they held back in the old country. The only flaw in the plan was a lack of quarry. So in 1855 European red foxes were shipped in and let loose. *Tally ho!*

In less than a century, this immensely adaptable species had spread over most of the continent. It has recently made it across Bass Strait to Tasmania, a previously fox-free state. Their success is due to both a lack of predators (not much feeds on adult foxes) and their varied diet. Foxes eat everything—small mammals, birds, lizards, eggs, insects and other invertebrates and fruit. They also won't turn up their noses at garbage. And if they can get into the hen house, they'll dine like royalty.

Pal or pest?

How do I deal with them?

They are experts at raiding aviaries and chicken pens. Unless you own a chook-guarding Maremma dog, it's cheaper and simpler to protect the birds than it is to enclose the entire garden in fox-proof fencing (p. 208). Remember to run the mesh below ground to stop foxes (and other pests) digging their way in. You may also need to give the pen a roof or an overhang because foxes are expert climbers.

BATS

It doesn't matter if you don't have a belfry; bats might still move in with you.

Insect-eating bats are zippy little flitterers that come out at night to hunt insects. They communicate with each other through squeaks, but most of their calls are ultra high-pitched sounds that are beyond our hearing. They use this sonar to identify obstacles and pick out moths and beetles, which they catch in mid-air.

These furry fliers often move into attics and sheds—our equivalent of their natural haunts of caves and hollow trees. A small number of bats probably won't cause a problem, but a colony can produce a lot of wee and droppings. And a lot of waste brings in cockroaches and other pests.

Fruit bats or flying foxes look like large, slow-flapping birds in the night sky. Close up, flying foxes have long faces with big round eyes and constantly twitching ears. They gather in noisy, pongy roosts during the day where they squabble and squeal over space. At night, they're even more vocal when they find a source of food, such as a flowering gum or a mango tree.

Pal or pest?

A tricky one. Pals most of the time.
Flying foxes are pests if they're raiding your fruit trees or roosting next door. Insect-eaters are pests if they move in with you.

How do I deal with them?

Microbats are excellent at picking off flying insects, including mosquitoes and moths. Encourage them to lodge in your garden by putting up 'bat boxes', the batty version of nest boxes. Keep them away from the house or your new friends might decide that they've found a better option.

Block up access points to your roof space, if there's a chance that microbats might move in. This is much easier than evicting them. If microbats have already taken up residence inside your house, call in the bat experts.

Flying foxes can be noisy neighbours, especially if several thousand are roosting together. They pong and pinch your fruit. Some species are nomadic and will move on after a few loud and smelly months, unless there's a permanent food supply. Relocating a bat camp is extremely difficult. Melbourne achieved it with a high degree of success but not without a prolonged effort and a lot of tension between people and institutions.

Netting trees that are coming into fruit will reduce loss to bats and might also encourage the bats to move on. If you adopt this solution, ensure that the netting does not trap bats and birds.

Bats are implicated in the spread of a virus called lyssavirus, which is passed to humans by bites or scratches.

Flying foxes are also associated with Hendra virus, which is transmitted to horses. If you are bitten or scratched by a bat, wash the wound with soapy water, treat it with antiseptic and cover it with a dressing. Report the bite to a doctor, who will advise on further treatment. Although transmission is rare, it's not worth taking the risk of leaving a bite untreated.

BLACKBIRDS

Blackbirds are lurkers. They skulk in the undergrowth or hop cautiously around the garden on the lookout for the next meal. When alarmed, they give a loud *chuck-chuck-chuck* call as they scamper into the bushes or fly up into a tree. Another, altogether more annoying blackbird activity is digging, which uproots seedlings and redistributes mulch. They're after insects and other ground-dwelling Spineless. They are also partial to fruit.

Only male blackbirds are actually black. Their inky plumage is jazzed up with a golden beak and matching rings around the eyes. Females and young birds are dusty brown. It's a much better colour for camouflage.

Native to Europe, they were introduced by settlers to bring the sound of home to the Australian bush. Blackbirds are now widespread in gardens and parks in the southeast including Tasmania.

Pal or pest?

They eat destructive insects but they're pests when they dig up the vegie patch and redecorate the garden.

How do I deal with them?

It's difficult to target blackbirds without affecting other species. Protective netting, which is effective for most problem birds, doesn't work with blackbirds because the little lurkers sneak in under the edges. Visual scarers may be more successful. Try balloons painted with big staring eyes and decorated with dangling ribbons.

STARLINGS

Is there a medium-sized black bird on your television aerial? Does it have an iridescent sheen, mottling on its breast and wings, a narrow beak and a lively call? Then it's probably a common starling. The native metallic starling of North Queensland has a long tail and red eyes.

Like other introduced birds, starlings associate with people. They feed on fruit, grain and insects. Their fruit- and grain-eating activities cause real problems for farmers. As well as raiding crops, they also uncover planted grain and steal stock feed. Because the birds travel in large flocks, the effect can be severe. They also nest in tree hollows, either competing with native birds or evicting them. And they poo on everything.

They are entrenched in much of the southeast corner of Australia, with smaller numbers in North Queensland and on the Nullarbor Plain. Occasionally, they pop up on the other side of the Nullarbor, where the Agricultural Protection Board and other government bodies take care of them as soon as they are spotted. Even so, they are slowly spreading towards the southwestern wheatbelt.

Pal or pest?

How do I deal with them?

Cover fruit trees with nets (p. 208) to stop the birds raiding them. If starlings are persistent, you may have to find a way of scaring them repeatedly until they give up and leave to find an easier target (suggestions on p. 216). Block off access points to your roof to keep them out.

KOELS AND SPANGLED DRONGOS

If you live along the north or east coast, you've probably been kept awake by a koel. Males call at night with a relentlessly repeated *ko-el* and an even more maddening series of rising whistles. Koels are heard more often than they're seen. Males are sleek and black with a long, blunt-ended tail. Females and young birds are brown with lighter spots and streaks.

Spangled drongos are also black but have a long forked tail. These birds behave as if they've had too much coffee, chattering, squeaking and twanging like wire. Koels and drongos have bright red eyes.

Both species migrate: koels between New Guinea and Australia, drongos within Australia. In spring, they fly south to breed. They head back north in autumn.

When looking for mates, male koels call day and night. It's enough to drive the sensitive to earplugs. Or drink. Or both. Fortunately, the birds are not so noisy when they've finished breeding. Koels also have another odd habitat—they lay their eggs in other birds' nests.

Drongos don't take the same liberties with their neighbours' property but they are aggressive towards other birds.

Pal or pest?
That depends on whether or not you're a light sleeper.

How do I deal with them?

Koels are a real problem only during the breeding season. It's difficult to persuade birds to move on, so foam earplugs may be the most effective solution.

RAVENS AND CROWS

The Australian raven has taken to towns in a big way. You can see groups of them in parks and ovals, picnic grounds and roadsides, investigating every possible source of food. They also pick through paddocks on the lookout for beetle grubs or raid market gardens and orchards. In many places, ravens are happy to be around people.

Ravens and crows are big glossy black birds with hefty beaks and pale eyes. It can take practice to distinguish between them. (It was only about 40 years ago that we realised that five species lived in Australia, not three, as previously thought. Even the professionals have problems telling them apart!)

The Australian raven has a beard of long feathers (throat hackles), which spread out while calling. You'll know the call: a far-carrying *aah-aah-aah-aaaahhhh*, with a extended and cracked last note, and a drawn-out, desolate wail.

Other species of ravens and crows lack throat hackles. The little raven lives in the southeast, whereas the forest raven is the local bird for most Tasmanians. Torresian crows are northerners. The little crow, the smallest of the five species, occurs over much of inland Australia. It is often very tame around people.

Pal or pest?
Mostly pal but they have some pesty habits. The call of the Australian raven can drive some people to distraction! They also raid rubbish bins.

How do I deal with them?

Don't feed them. Keep lids on bins to stop the birds redistributing rubbish. Clean up fallen fruit and pet food. They will soon move on if there's nothing for them to eat.

MAGPIES

For most of the year, magpies are good-natured neighbours. Their complex melodies of trills and warbles are a characteristic sound of Australia from the cities to the outback. Magpies feed on invertebrates, lizards, frogs—just about anything else that will fit into a beak. They are usually great pals in the garden.

But in the breeding season, they turn fiercely protective of their young. Magpies swoop on passersby with a rustling of wings that'll give you a fright. And the birds are persistent. If you don't move on quickly enough they will sometimes make contact with their feet or beak. Now *that* will get the desired reaction. This aggressive behaviour gets dangerous if they scare someone into running out into traffic.

Pal or pest?

Pal for most of the time. Pest for a brief period during the breeding season.

How do I deal with them?

Every year, local councils and government departments are inundated with requests to deal with the problem of swooping magpies. Suggestions abound. Wear a cycling helmet with big eyes painted on it, carry an umbrella or stare down the bird. All have merit but it takes a strong will to carry on unperturbed when a big black and white bird launches itself at your head. Alternative suggestions include using a dog as a decoy. (This does seem a bit mean to the dog.) Perhaps the only foolproof solution—one that helps both you and the birds—is to find another path until the nesters are through.

BUTCHERBIRDS, CURRAWONGS AND WHITE-WINGED CHOUGHS

Australia is home to a surprisingly large number of black and white birds that visit parks, suburban gardens and bush blocks. It's easy to sort them out once you get your eye in, but that can take a bit of practice.

Start by crossing magpies off the list. You already know those. Butcherbirds have black heads, white bellies and two-toned beaks. Like magpies, they are great singers. They will often call at night, if the moonlight is bright enough. While their songs are beautiful, their table manners are not quite so pleasant. Butcherbirds eat anything they can kill. If the prey is too big to swallow whole, they will jam it into the fork of a tree and tear it apart with their hooked beaks. They will also store food for later on. Waste not, want not.

Currawongs are black or grey with white markings on the tail. Their yellow eyes give them an intense stare. These inquisitive birds are also known as bell-magpies because of their spirited, almost metallic ringing and chiming songs. Currawongs dig up lawns and peel away tree bark to get at curl grubs (p. 32). They love stick insects (p. 95) and will gather in flocks to feed when stick insects are around in large numbers. Unfortunately, they will also raid unattended nests for eggs or chicks.

White-winged choughs are black birds with white crescents on their wings, curved black beaks and crimson irises with a mad look. Choughs are nowhere near as musical as currawongs and butcherbirds. A plaintive whistle and a hiss is as melodic as they get.

They are sociable birds, congregating in small mobs, raking over carefully placed mulch and digging up soil for insects and other invertebrates.

Pal or pest?

How do I deal with them?

Don't feed them and they won't hang around to mooch, although they will still help themselves to pest insects, especially beetle larvae. Plant thick vegetation to protect other birds' nests from currawong raids.

MAGPIE-LARKS

Magpie-larks are noisy birds with snazzy black and white plumage. Males have a black bib and a horizontal black line through the eye. Females have a white bib (outlined in black) and a vertical black eye line. They strut like a sergeant-major with a lot of head-bobbing. Calls are strident and sharp. Pairs often duet with one calling 'zee-zee' followed by its mate adding 'pee-wit'.

They're also known as Murray magpies, mudlarks (after their fondness for mud as a building material) and peewits or peewees (after their calls).

They construct their cup-shaped nests out of mud and grass, usually on a horizontal branch. During the breeding season, pairs engage in aerial dogfights with other birds. Males often get shirty with their reflections in windows or mirrors and try to chase off the intruders. This involves a lot of droppings, which invariable end up on car roofs or window sills. Nesting birds are loud and scolding and will occasionally swoop on people.

Pal or pest?

How do I deal with them?

Cover wing mirrors and windscreens to stop magpie-lark attacks on parked cars. If nesting birds get aggressive, try some of the anti-magpie tricks, such as wearing a hat with eyes or carrying an umbrella.

WILLIE WAGTAILS

These energetic birds wag their tails from side to side, darting out from a perch to snatch flies from the air. They're not shy. Willie wagtails will even follow you about while you're gardening to pick up any insects you disturb as you work.

You can't miss them. They are stylish black and white birds with long white eyebrows. You'll often hear their trilling, rolling calls on moonlit nights. (Do they *ever* sleep?) During the breeding season, they weave neat little nests from grass stems and bark fibres. They are covered on the outside with spiders' webs and lined with down, wool and animal hair. Wagtail chicks have a cosy start to life.

Adults may dive-bomb you in an attempt to keep you away from the nest. They are astonishingly game little birds, given the difference in size between attacker and attacked. Their fluttering and swooping is usually preceded by a harsh, rattling alarm call—so don't say you haven't been warned.

Pal or pest?

How do I deal with them?

Willie wagtails like a mix of shrubs and lawn. They prefer to hunt in open spaces. Because they are voracious insect eaters, avoid using pest sprays and other treatments unless absolutely necessary. If you're feeling particularly generous, you can provide them with bits of wool collected from sheep farm fences, so their chicks can grow up in comfort.

COMMON MYNAS

Mynas strut around as though they own the place. They almost do. Bold and aggressive birds, mynas beat up other species and chase them away. When they move in, others move out.

Dapper birds, they are outfitted in brown and black plumage with white wing spots, gold beaks and gold marks around the eyes. They are also very vocal, communicating with one another in a wide range of croaks, whistles and trills. Although their names sound the same, they are not related to noisy miners. Mynas are a type of starling, whereas miners are native honeyeaters (p. 168). (Confusingly, noisy miners also have gold beaks and gold around the eyes . . .)

Mynas hail from southern Asia. They were brought into Australia as a way of controlling flies at the Melbourne saleyards. This attempt at biological control went horribly wrong. The flies are still there and the mynas have moved on. They are now found in major towns along the east coast from Melbourne to Cairns.

Pal or pest?

How do I deal with them?

Feeding encourages pest birds, so drop the stale bread into the worm farm or bury it in the compost heap rather than chucking it to the mynas. Block access points to your roof and gutter to prevent nesting. Check with your local council about myna control programs in your area. If you build your own traps, be aware that they may also catch native birds so monitor them closely. Ensure that trapped mynas are euthanised humanely.

SPARROWS

Sparrows are bold, little brown and grey birds that like to hang around with people. Their persistent *cheep-cheep-cheep* call is a sound of eastern towns. The house sparrow is seen most often. Males have a chestnut brown head and mottled wings, grey cap and front, white cheeks and a black bib. Females are mottled brown. Tree sparrows are similar but sport a chestnut cap and a black bib and black patches on the cheeks. Males and females are identical.

House sparrows occur in the eastern half of the country but tree sparrows are restricted to Victoria and southern New South Wales. Both species were introduced into Australia in the 1860s.

City sparrows are street urchins straight out of Dickens. Watching them steal crumbs from table tops in shopping malls, it's difficult not to picture a sparrow Fagin somewhere in the background. Rural sparrows feed on fruit and grain, which they also spoil with their droppings. Although they build nests just about anywhere, tree hollows are a favourite spot. They compete for these with native birds. They may also block gutters with their nests.

Pal or pest?

How do I deal with them?

Don't feed sparrows because one or two will turn into dozens in no time at all. Block up access points to your roof space and consider covering your gutters with a leaf guard to stop them building nests. Keep an eye on nest boxes because sparrows will take over.

NOISY MINERS AND BELLBIRDS

Not to be confused with the introduced common myna (p. 165), miners are native honeyeaters. They're small birds with big characters. And when a gang of them move into the neighbourhood, they make their presence known.

Noisy miners and yellow-throated miners are grey and brown birds with golden beaks and a patch of gold behind each eye. Their close relatives, the bellbirds or bell miners are olive green with a red-gold beak and eye patch. You're more likely to hear bellbirds than see them. The piercing *tink* is a familiar sound in southeastern parks and forests. Don't stand too close!

Miners have benefitted from our plantings of native species in parks and gardens. They feed on nectar and insects but are fiercely territorial and will chase away other species. Unfortunately, they have a big impact on other insect-eating birds. It seems that wherever the miners take over, the number of insect-eaters decline. You can see the problem.

Pal or pest?
Pest in large numbers.

How do I deal with them?

Plant shrubs to provide cover for smaller insect-eating birds. This lets them escape from miners that are staking out a territory. The bullies prefer a mix of trees and grasses and are not so sure of themselves when the vegetation is more tangled. It might be possible to control miner abundance by cutting down on nectar-rich plants, but other species will suffer too.

WATTLEBIRDS AND FRIARBIRDS

Wattlebirds and friarbirds have done very well from the shift towards planting native flowers in gardens. They are honeyeaters, relying on flowers for their food. In the bush, they are nomadic, moving from place to place as one type of plant stops flowering and another starts. A wanderer's life is one of constant searching. Where's the next meal coming from?

But the profusion of grevilleas, banksias and other nectar-rich species in parks and gardens allow the birds to settle down in one place. No more roaming. Dinner is served.

Despite their quarrelsome natures, red wattlebirds live cheek by jowl in urban areas across southern Australia. If you don't spot these plump, brown mottled, yellow-bellied honeyeaters as they chase one another out of trees, you'll certainly hear their conversational cackles and ringing *wok-wok-wok-wok*. They're missing from Tasmania, which is home to yellow wattlebirds.

With their weird and complex calls, grey feathers and bald black heads, friarbirds are not easy to confuse with anything else. When they get together in flowering trees, you can hear the racket from a long way away.

Pal or pest?
Pal, although they can scare away smaller birds from feeding sites. Friarbirds may be pests in orchards.

How do I deal with them?

Plant native trees and shrubs to encourage them. (Not that wattlebirds need much encouragement.) Smaller nectar-eating birds will welcome dense or spiny vegetation that let them through while keeping out the bulkier birds.

FINCHES AND FAIRY-WRENS

You hear flocks of finches and wrens before you see them. These tiny, colourful birds make a big noise when they gather to feed. Finches like long grasses that have gone to seed. Wrens forage for insects in bushes and among tall flowers. Where there's one, there'll be others.

Zebra finches, common in drier areas, are fawn with bright orange beaks and black and white striped tails. Red-browed finches of the southeast have crimson eyebrows that give them a very serious expression. Tropical double-barred finches are white-bellied birds with two black lines across their fronts. Other species come in browns, greens and reds.

During the spring and summer breeding season, male superb and splendid blue wrens are startling shades of sapphire and cobalt. You can't miss them as they hop along on the lookout for creepy crawlies. At other times, they resemble the females in a much more subtle buff with a dusty blue sheen on the tail.

Pal or pest?

How do I deal with them?

Encourage finches by growing native grasses. As insect eaters, wrens will appreciate densely growing flowering shrubs that attract flies and bugs. Give them a bird bath that is safe from cats and they will make great use of it. You can buy or make nest boxes or baskets, or roll up steel or plastic mesh into a cylinder, add some strips of paperbark and hang it somewhere away from predators. They will ditch the contents or rearrange them to suit. Some birds are impossibly house-proud.

PARDALOTES

Pardalotes are active little birds that spend part of their day searching gum trees for insects and part of it burrowing in soil. If you spot a light brown, black and yellow ball of feathers flying up from the ground into a tree, look carefully at the spot vacated by the bird. If you're lucky, you'll find the entrance to a tunnel. This leads into the pardalote's nest—these cute little birds regularly build their homes underground.

Three types of pardalotes are commonly found in woodland, parks and gardens Australia. All are between 8 and 12 cm long with buff or grey backs, paler tummies and dark wings.

Striated pardalotes live all over the country, wherever there is a good supply of their favourite food: scale insects (see p. 198). In the tropics, they have black caps but elsewhere the tops of their heads are covered in narrow stripes (striations). Spotted pardalotes have black wings, yellow throats and yellow or orange rumps. Red-browed pardalotes are more sombre, with grey and yellow wings. Both types have white dots on their scones.

Pardalotes build their nests in earth or sand, especially in riverbanks and road cuttings. That pile of top soil you've been meaning to move? It's pardalote heaven.

Pal or pest?

How do I deal with them?

Build or buy nest boxes to encourage them to stay in your garden. If they've taken over the earth or sand pile, consider leaving it alone until the young have left.

PIGEONS AND DOVES

You know spring is here when pigeons start strutting their stuff. All over the country, male birds puff out their chests, fan their tails and bow to prospective mates. They accompany their displays with cooing songs.

Australia has about two dozen different species of pigeons and doves, most of them native. Introduced species are common in the south. Since their arrival in the early days of settlement, feral pigeons or rock doves have spread out from towns into rural areas. In the wild, they nest on rock ledges. Window sills, roof tops and gutters are even better. No wonder feral pigeons do so well around people.

Two other species have been introduced. The spotted turtle dove is very common in parks and gardens along the east coast and the southwest. Western Australia also has the laughing turtle dove, a small bird with a brown and black band on its throat.

Native species have also taken to the rich pickings of gardens and parks. A few years ago, crested pigeons were birds of farms and grasslands, but now they've moved into cities. Tiny peaceful doves are either very relaxed or confident in their camouflage because they often stay put as you approach. It is easy to miss them until they take flight—sometimes only a metre away. In rainforest areas, emerald or green-winged pigeons are always on the lookout for fallen fruit.

Pal or pest?
Feral pigeons are pests.

How do I deal with them?

Don't feed feral pigeons. Destroy nests as the birds build them. Because pigeons are persistent—they didn't reach *those* numbers by giving up easily—you may need to do this repeatedly before they move on. Block access to your roof and cover gutters to keep them out.

COCKATOOS

If anything says 'Australia', it's a sulphur-crested cockatoo. Literally and figuratively, as it happens, because cockatoos are kept as companion animals the world over for their speaking skills and engaging natures. The cockatoos are another group that's a speciality of the continent. Although they also occur in New Guinea, Indonesia and the Philippines, nowhere else has so many species. When it comes to cockatoos, we rock.

That's not to say that our relationship with them is always smooth. Cockatoos are mischievous birds and sometimes they play rough. Sulphur-crested cockatoos, in particular, entertain themselves by demolishing exposed woodwork on buildings. Beaks that can crack hakea pods make short work of sawn timber.

Once birds of gum forests and open land, galahs and corellas are now at home in the suburbs, where they dig up lawns and golf courses to pick out plant bulbs. Out in the bush, black cockatoos feed on she-oak cones, but they also flock to pine plantations to dine on seeds. In the southeast, gang-gang cockatoos visit gardens for hawthorn and other introduced berries and fruits.

Pal or pest?
That depends on what they're doing. All species can destroy property when they put their minds to it.

How do I deal with them?

Destructive birds may be killing time between feeds. If you're the one feeding them, you know what you have to do. If they're still hanging around, wires stretched a couple of centimetres above landing spots may discourage them from settling.

LORIKEETS

Almost everything about lorikeets is frantic. They zip between trees, flapping their wings like crazy. When eating or flying, they call to each other in whistles and shrieks. You know when lorikeets are around. Even if you can't see them, you can hear them. There's nothing low key about these nectar-feeding parrots.

Most lorikeets are nomads. They follow the blossom. On spotting a tree in flower, they land and sop up the nectar with brush-like tongues. Other lorikeets home in on the calls. In no time, a flowering tree can be rustling with dozens of these colourful parrots.

Spectacular in green, blue and red, rainbow lorikeets are the most familiar of these birds. They have taken advantage of native trees planted in urban streets and moved into areas where they previously didn't occur.

The smaller birds are musk lorikeets in the southeast including Tasmania, purple-crowned lorikeets in the south, and varied lorikeets in the Top End.

Pal or pest?

They're pals because they pollinate trees. But they can become pests if they settle in around a permanent food source.

How do I deal with them?

Don't feed lorikeets unless you (and your neighbours) are prepared to put up with their early morning wake-up shrieks and gloopy poo. If you want lorikeets in your garden, it's best to entertain them as visitors. Plant flowering trees—they love gums and grevilleas—and put up nest boxes. They'll stay a while and move on.

OTHER PARROTS

If Australia voted on a favourite parrot, the winner would be a rosella. No contest. These mild-mannered, multicoloured birds occur over most of the continent. The most familiar are the eastern and crimson rosellas of the east coast, but there's a different type for every city. Tasmania has green rosellas, Townsville and Brisbane have pale-headed rosellas,

Darwin northern and Perth western rosellas. The colours vary, but they all have long tails, scalloped patterns on their backs and wings and distinct cheek patches.

Scarlet and emerald-coloured king parrots are common visitors to gardens near parks and woodlands. If you live in a drier area, you might host small groups of red-rumped parrots. Males are brilliant green with a crimson patch on the back, whereas females are a modest olive.

Different versions of the ringneck, Port Lincoln or 28 parrot are found in inland and southwestern Australia. In some places, they descend on orchards and vineyards in large flocks and strip fruit. Next to the cockatoos, they are probably the most intrusive of our native parrots.

Pal or pest?

Pal. Ringneck parrots can be pests in orchards.

How do I deal with them?

Encourage parrots by leaving dead trees in which they can build their nests (as long as the trees are away from houses) or by putting nest boxes. Use netting (p. 209) to protect fruit from marauding ringnecks.

KOOKABURRAS

You know the call. It even pops up on the soundtrack of old Tarzan movies, although there are no kookaburras in Africa. In parks and gardens all over eastern Australia, the laughing kookaburra wakes up the neighbourhood with a distinctive hearty chuckle that builds into a maniacal cackle. When one begins, the others join in until the whole group is hooting with laughter. For overseas visitors, this is the quintessential sound of the Australian bush.

The laughing kookaburra is one of two types of kookaburra in Australia. (The other is the northern blue-winged kookaburra.) Both are hefty birds with long, sturdy beaks and serious expressions. The laughing kookaburra has a dark band through its eyes.

Kookaburras quickly get accustomed to people, especially in parks and gardens, which they learn are a source of handouts. They may get so bold that they steal food from a barbecue hotplate, picnic table or right out of your hand. They return to a nearby perch where they often beat the living daylights out of a sausage before swallowing it.

Pal or pest?

How do I deal with them?

Resist the urge to feed them because you may give them health problems through an unbalanced diet. Be careful with rat poisons and insecticides. They target pests that kookaburras eat. Instead, leave wild corners in the garden and perhaps build a compost heap, so there'll be plenty of creepy crawlies for them to eat.

SWALLOWS, MARTINS AND SWIFTS

Swallows, martins and swifts perform their aerobatic tricks around buildings and across open paddocks and roads. They're chasing insects—especially flies—which have a few aerial manoeuvres of their own. These little birds are flying aces.

Welcome swallows are found almost everywhere across the country. With their satiny blue-black backs and wings, rosy faces and Zorro masks, they are easy to identify. In flight, their white tummies and forked tails are characteristic. Swallows raise their young in nests made from mud and lined with grass and feathers for comfort. They often build their nests under eaves, where droppings can foul up walls and patios.

Fairy martins also nest close to humans. They live in colonies and build bottle-shaped mud nests around barns and houses. Once the young have left, the nests are sometimes taken over by pardalotes (p. 173) or wasps (p. 119). Fairy martins are identified by their russet caps, white rumps and square tails.

Swifts spend most of their adult lives in the air. They even sleep on the wing. Needletails often gather in large flocks to hunt insects—a spectacular sight as they swoop and glide on long, sickle wings.

Pal or pest?

Pals for eating flies. Loads of flies.
Pests when nesting in the wrong place.

How do I deal with them?

Fishing wire stretched tight across likely nesting places may deter birds. If using this method, make sure that the birds can't become caught up in it.

BRUSH TURKEYS

Unmistakeable, the brush turkey looks like a very big, black chook with huge feet, a bald red head and a yellow collar like a deflated balloon. If those aren't enough clues, the brush turkey's tail folds vertically.

These birds live in forests along the east coast, as far south as mid-New South Wales. In some areas, turkeys are thick on the ground, taking advantage of the plentiful food and protection provided by people.

Turkeys feed on whatever they can uncover with those enormous feet. A bird will industriously rake over the leaf litter, picking out morsels, and then rake it over again. Seedlings fall victim to the endless gardening, so young plants have no chance when turkeys are about. The birds also scrape mulch into a huge mound in which they incubate their eggs. Chicks can pretty much fend for themselves on hatching. They are small, podgy and brown-feathered at first, but soon take on the look of the adults.

Pal or pest?
A pest if you want to keep a tidy garden.

How do I deal with it?

Like all native birds, brush turkeys are protected, so as much as you'd like to do something *really decisive*, you can't. The first rule of control is: don't feed them. Providing handouts is a guarantee that your garden will turn into Brush Turkey Central.

If you can't keep them away, the best you can hope is to minimise damage. A mulch of pegged-down palm fronds can frustrate their activities.

BIRDS OF PREY

They fly so high that you can only just make out the forked tail of a black kite or the snow-white belly of a sea eagle. But although you can barely see them, they can pick up all the detail they need. Birds of prey have eyes that are at least six times better than ours at resolving images. But wait, there's more. Their eyes have a section that works like a built-in telephoto lens. Part of what they see is magnified compared with the rest of their view.

Australia is home to two dozen birds of prey. Some of the more common species are easily identified.

Wedge-tailed eagles are huge birds with a distinctive diamond-shaped tail. They are usually seen circling over farmland or feeding on roadkill. Roadsides are popular feeding places with nankeen kestrels and black-shouldered kites. They hover a few metres above the ground, searching for mice, lizards and large insects. Both have pale undersides (which is usually all you see of them as you drive past). The wings of black-shouldered kites are tipped with grey and have a black spot about halfway along. Those of nankeen kestrels are vaguely streaked.

Pal or pest?

How do I deal with them?

Chooks and ducks may prove too tempting a target for larger birds of prey, so make sure that domestic fowl have raptor-proof pens. A fully enclosed run is perfect, but a shelter will give your chooks a fighting chance.

OWLS

You might see one as a ghostly shape flying across the garden at night, but you usually have to be lucky, clued up or both to get a good look at an owl. A few species are common in parks and larger gardens—even in the cities—yet they are more often heard than seen. The boobook or morepork calls out its name. Barking owls give a double yap that sounds just like a small, noisy dog—if that small, noisy dog were stuck in a tree. Barn owls give a hoarse screech.

Owls are easily distinguished from other birds, although they are sometimes mistaken for frogmouths (see p. 189). They sit upright, have flat faces, short necks and round, forward-facing eyes. Frogmouths are a little less bookish and more streamlined.

Boobooks and barking owls have bright yellow eyes. Set against dark feathers and under white 'eyebrows', they give the birds a surprised expression. Barn owls have dark eyes in a heart-shaped white face. They seem to be more composed.

As night fliers, owls spend their days asleep in tree hollows or high among the branches. While they doze, smaller birds may gather together to try to make them move on. Owls, after all, are predators and potential prey doesn't differentiate between daylight and night-time hunters. A mob of shrieking, dive-bombing honeyeaters is often worth a closer look. It might indicate an owl in the tree.

Pal or pest?

How do I deal with them?

Owls don't often cause problems in domestic gardens but, if there's one around, it's a good idea to lock up your chooks or guinea pigs at night. Just in case.

FROGMOUTHS

Frogmouths sleep during the day. They sit motionless on branches, relying on their brown and grey feathers to conceal them against the tree bark. Despite their size—they are as big as magpies, although not quite as streamlined—you might easily miss a snoozing frogmouth, even in broad daylight.

If it knows it's been spotted, a frogmouth will strike a 'broken branch' pose. The bird stretches out, beak pointed up, feathers smooth and flat, so it resembles a shattered tree limb. The eyes might look as though they're closed but the frogmouth watches from under feathered lids. If you move, the bird will turn its head, very slowly, to follow you. The broken branch pose is good but it isn't perfect.

At night, frogmouths become hunters. They perch in the open, often on fence posts, to watch for cockroaches, moths and beetles. Lizards, frogs and the occasional small mouse end up on the menu too. Frogmouths will eat anything they can fit into their beaks.

Because of their huge, golden eyes, hooked beaks and nocturnal habits, they are often mistaken for owls (p. 187). They can be difficult to tell apart, but a frogmouth has a flattish head, eyes that don't point directly forward and a wide beak. How wide? As wide as a frog's mouth, of course.

Pal or pest?
They eat insects, including cockroaches.

How do I deal with them?

Frogmouths hunting on roads are sometimes hit by cars, so take care when driving at night. If you find an injured bird, take it to a local vet or wildlife carer.

MASKED LAPWINGS OR SPUR-WINGED PLOVERS

With their yellow superhero face-wear, salmon-pink legs and snooty manners, masked lapwings are unmistakeable. Even their calls are distinct—a peevish, high-pitched *kekekekek* that carries a long way, especially at night. If that isn't distinctive enough, they have a sharp, forward-pointing spike on the front of each wing. (Their alternative name of spur-winged plovers is taken from this.) They are odd birds, indeed.

Lapwings are birds of open ground. They nest wherever there is a good supply of food and no overhanging vegetation. In the wild, they roam along beaches and the edges of swamps, but in towns they prefer lawns and parks, roadside verges and golf courses. Their choices can make their lives—and everyone else's—difficult, during the breeding season at least.

For most of the year, plovers are slightly grumpy neighbours. They might give you a bit of a look as you pass by, but they won't front up. But during the breeding season, the story changes. Plovers are very defensive of their chicks so they will attempt to drive away intruders by swooping on them and shrieking. They will even take on 4WD vehicles. Luckily for all concerned, plovers usually don't make contact with their targets.

Pal or pest?
A pal for most of the year but a pest when they've got chicks.

How do I deal with them?

Dive-bombing plovers are almost impossible to deter, so the simplest solution is to keep out of their way during the breeding period. Your council may be able to provide specific advice.

WHITE IBIS

The white ibis is a large bird with a very long curved beak. Ibis feathers are mostly white but those on the tummy are usually stained with mud—or worse. (Ibis don't dine at the best restaurants.) You can't mistake these birds for anything else. If it has a bald, black head coloured with a glimmer of purple across the nape and a lacy fan of black feathers near the tail, it's a white ibis.

The birds are found over most of the east and north of the continent and in the southwest of Western Australia, sometimes in very large flocks. They rarely wander across Bass Strait to Tasmania.

White ibis search for Spineless tidbits in paddocks, parks and swamps. Their long beaks probe the mud for worms and beetle larvae. White ibis also rummage through rubbish tips. In city parks, they quickly learn that humans are a source of handouts. Bolder birds may turn into standover merchants, menacing small children into surrendering their sandwiches.

A related species, the straw-necked ibis, has iridescent purple-green wings and head and long, pale yellow feathers on its throat. Straw-necked ibises visit parks and playing fields but don't mingle with humans to the same extent as white ibises. They usually don't steal your lunch.

Pal or pest?
White ibis can be pests around people but pals in the paddock.

How do I deal with them?

Don't encourage them by feeding them in parks or gardens.

MOORHENS, COOTS AND SWAMPHENS

As bald as a coot—as a simile goes, it's not very good. Coots are as fully feathered as any of their kin. Like the moorhens and swamphens, they have a shield—a featherless plate that extends from the beak to the forehead—but does that make them 'bald'? And if so, why not point a finger at the moorhens too? Coots catch all the flak.

These birds that dress in sombre colours. Coots wear basic black set off with a white beak and forehead shield and grey legs. Moorhens are dusky brown, with a yellow-tipped red beak, a red shield and pinkish legs. They also have a flash of white feathers under the tail, which is sometimes all you see as they disappear into the reeds.

Swamphens look like oversized moorhens but are much showier. They have royal blue or purple belly and neck and dark back and wings. Beak and shield are bright red and the legs are pink. Swamphens also have white backsides.

Another bird in this group, the native-hen, also resembles the moorhen with dark plumage and yellow-green and red beak. You can tell them apart by the white spots on the native-hen's sides, its bright red legs and black bottom.

And not one of them is bald.

Pal or pest?
Pal (in small numbers).

How do I deal with them?

If they are making a nuisance of themselves by covering your lawn and paths in slimy poo, encourage them to move on by clearing away long grass and placing a screen around your pond or swimming pool.

WEIRD STUFF

LEAF MINERS

Scribbles in leaves are the work of leaf mining insects, especially moths. Beetles, flies and wasps also mine leaves.

For many insects, the leaves are the choicest part of a plant. The tissue inside a leaf is sweet and juicy, but it's covered by a sturdy layer of skin. It's too tough for small jaws to snip through over and over again. So for the tiniest leaf-eaters, once is enough.

Leaf miners bite into the leaf's skin, opening up a hole just big enough to slip under. Once inside, they tunnel through the tissue. Because the leaf's skin is transparent, the insect's travels are marked out by the dead cells. There's a dual advantage for the insects: not only does the leaf provide food but the skin that protects the leaf's innards from damage and drying out also protects the tiny insects.

They eat the tissue or suck the sap that flows through the leaf's veins. The mines look silver because there's nothing between the two layers of skin. Up close, you might notice a thread running through the tunnels. It's leaf miner poo.

Leaf-mining flies have been introduced to help control

the pest plant lantana. Although the flies don't kill lantana, their activity slows its growth. A moth has also been introduced to combat the pasture weed Paterson's curse.

Pal or pest?
If they're mining one of your prized plants—pest!

How do I deal with them?

Spray leaves with white oil (p. 218) to kill leaf miners.

LEAF SKELETONISERS

Some insects eat only the green parts of a leaf, avoiding the tough, chewy veins. These finicky eaters reduce leaves to skeletons while they are still attached to the plant.

Judging by the numbers of lacy remnants dangling from trees, a lot of insects feed this way. Cherry or pear slugs (p. 23) are among the most common of the leaf skeletonisers. They dine on fruit trees and ornamentals.

Some native moth caterpillars also feed in this way. Autumn gum moth caterpillars dine at night, spending their days hidden in a silk-wrapped shelter of leaves at the end of a stem. The hairy gumleaf skeletonising caterpillar is another choosy eater. These odd little insects are easy to identify. Every time one sheds its skin, it holds on to the empty head capsule. After a few moultings, it ends up carrying a stack of them on its head—earning it the nickname the Mad Haterpillar.

Pal or pest?
Skeletonisers are pests in large numbers.

How do I deal with them?

See p. 24 for suggestions on controlling cherry slugs. Caterpillars are sometimes more difficult to control with pest sprays. Those of the autumn gum moth are tucked away by day, so avoid direct contact with spray. The furry covering of the hairy gumleaf skeletonising caterpillars makes it difficult for the spray to do its work. Either pick off the caterpillars by hand (wearing gloves) or apply Bt or the natural insecticide *spinosad* to affected plants.

SCABS AND SCALES

If your plants look as though they've got a bad case of chickenpox, they've probably been infested by scale insects. These tiny relatives of white flies and aphids (p. 74) hide under miniature shields made of wax. Beneath this protective casing, they feed on leaf sap. One or two scale insects don't cause problems. One or two thousand is another matter altogether.

Scale insects have an unusual life history. Only females live under cover. They are strange-looking insects even by the high standards set by their fellow bugs. Wingless and legless, they are permanently attached to their food source by the rostrum, the needle-like mouthparts through which they suck up sap. Males have wings and resemble midges.

Scale insects are amazingly prolific breeders. A female can produce up to a thousand eggs. Given that there may be as many as six generations a year, that's . . . well . . . *a lot* of children, grandchildren, great-grandchildren. Billions. Luckily, most of them don't survive to adulthood, otherwise we'd be drowning in scale insects. Even their ant carers can't protect them all (p. 62).

Pal or pest?
Pest. Large infestations cause leaf drop.

How do I deal with them?

The waxy shield protects adult females from most sprays, but white oil and garlic spray will knock off mobile young. (Remember that those sprays will also affect other insects.) Predatory mites, antlions and ladybirds feed on scale. Encouraging these will help to control the problem.

BAGS AND CASES

Some caterpillars weave sleeping-bags in which they doze all day. These bags are made of web and hairs that have come loose from the caterpillars. They are ace recyclers.

Caterpillars of the bag-shelter or processionary moth share a communal case that lies at the base of their food tree or up among its branches. Because a few dozen caterpillars squash in together, the retreat soon becomes as messy as a teenager's bedroom. The caterpillars feed at night. Each evening, a few climb up the tree, paying out a silk thread that guides others to food. They crawl up the tree in single file. After having their fill of wattle leaves, they return to the bag-shelter, where they spend the day, hidden from predators.

Other caterpillars, especially those of the moth family Psychidae, produce individual bags, which they decorate with leaf fragments or twigs. They line up the pieces in an orderly fashion. The results are often exquisite constructions that are well hidden on trees and shrubs. Some species buck the trend for neatness and plaster the cases with their poo. Each to its own.

Pal or pest?
Most species don't do much damage in small numbers.

How do I deal with them?

If you need to remove them, always wear gloves and be careful about breathing in the silk and hairs or getting them into your eyes. Don't put your hands near your face after handling the bags. If you do experience a bad reaction, seek medical assistance.

LUMPS AND BUMPS

Sometimes plants are afflicted with the sorts of lumps and bumps that turn them into the green equivalent of the Elephant Man. Tiny vases project from leaves. Stems swell up with protuberances that look like unripe fruit. It's not a pretty sight, but it is a curious one.

Galls are a plant's response to insect damage. When insects or fungi attack, a plant sometimes responds by producing galls. This is a local growth of tissue that often takes a characteristic form that varies with the attacking species.

Most galls occur on leaves. Tiny wasps are responsible for the greatest diversity—pimples, buttons, cones and blisters. Bugs also have an impact. The scale insect *Apiomorpha* produces different types of gall on gum trees. In one species, male galls are tubular, often with a trumpet-like flared opening, whereas female galls look like small avocados. In other species, galls may have long spiny projections.

Pal or pest?
They're unsightly but don't do lasting damage to healthy plants.

How do I deal with them?

It is difficult to control gall-forming insects because they are protected by the gall. Natural control includes parasitoid wasps, which lay their eggs on the insects. You can also destroy the galls when they form to interrupt the life cycle, but this may be messier than leaving them in place.

MUD CHIMNEYS

First, holes appear in the lawn. They're not the pencil-thin burrows of wolf spiders. They might belong to cicadas (p. 71) but you can't find their shed skins stuck to trees. Then chimneys grow around the holes. They're made of mud, heaped together in dollops. What made them? Ants? Earthworms?

Have you considered crayfish? The chimneys are the entrances to their burrows. These land-living relatives of yabbies and marrons usually tunnel into waterlogged soil near creeks and dams, although a few species prefer drier spots. (These rely on rain to keep their homes nice and damp.) Some of those tunnels may be as much as 10 m long. No mean feat for an animal that's no more than 45 mm from one end to the other.

The crayfish eat what they find as they mine the soil—anything from plant roots to worms. They emerge at night to get rid of the excavated dirt. Sticking the waste together creates the rustic-looking chimneys, which may be up to 40 cm tall.

Pal or pest?
If you're proud of your lawn, the chimneys might look messy. Large numbers can be a problem when mowing.

How do I deal with them?

There's not much you can do to evict them. If you knock down the chimneys, they'll simply build them up again. Draining the area will make it less attractive to the crayfish.

KEEPING PESTS UNDER CONTROL

BIOLOGICAL CONTROL

An animal's gotta eat. Caterpillars feed on plants. Spiders feed on caterpillars. Birds feed on spiders. You know the story. That's the simple version, of course. Even in the garden, with its limited range of species, the flow chart of who eats who is enormously complicated. Biological control is a technique that takes advantage of this food chain to keep pests in check. Instead of using chemicals to knock off the nuisances, it employs natural predators and parasites.

Biological control has received both good and bad press over the years. We all know about the introduction of cane toads into Australia as an example of biological control gone horribly wrong. (Bringing in common mynas wasn't exactly a triumph either.) But there have been many successes. When the Australian cottony cushion scale was accidentally introduced into California in the 1860s, it had a devastating impact on citrus production. After researching predators in the scale's natural habitat, scientists sent over the vedalia beetle and a parasitic fly to control it. They ate their way into the history books by saving the Californian citrus industry.

Biological control works on large-scale farms, but it can work in the garden too. Because each species tends to feed on a small number of different pests, it's important to match up predator with prey. This tight association reduces the chance of biological control going wrong, cane toad-style.

Predatory mites (p. 56) and parasitic wasps (p. 119) are bred in commercial operations to supply fruit and vegetable growers, but are often available in smaller quantities. Among those handy for gardens are the mites *Phytoseiulus* and *Typhlodromus*, which feed on eggs and adults of pest mites, and the wasps *Encarsia*, *Aphidius* and *Trichogramma* for white fly, aphids and fruit-eating caterpillars. Although this isn't the cheapest method of keeping pests in line—you'll need different critters for each target—it is very effective.

Other biological control agents work on a wider range of pests. When mixed with water and sprayed over plants, the bacterium Bt (*Bacillus thuringiensis*) kills leaf-eating caterpillars. It affects the caterpillar's gut, so it must be consumed to be effective. That means it doesn't knock off innocent bystanders that get caught in the spray, which is often a problem with even the mildest of chemical controls. Within a day of swallowing Bt as a topping on its leafy meal, the pest stops feeding. Not long after that, it turns up its multiple toes. Bt is available from gardening and hardware stores under the commercial name Dipel.

Ladybirds (p. 67), shield and assassin bugs (p. 72), lacewings (p. 111) and larval hoverflies (p. 104) are proficient pest-killers. They feed on aphids, caterpillars and other miniature nuisances. Some include insect eggs in their diets.

Whereas these take care of the leaf-crawlers, centipedes mop up the pests on the ground and web-building spiders snare them in mid-air. That's quite a team. And we haven't even started on the non-Spineless biological controls. All those frogs, lizards, birds and mammals have to eat *something*, don't they?

Encourage a variety of predators by maintaining some 'wild' spots in the garden. Also be very careful in any use of sprays and remedies mentioned in the next section because you might end up controlling the good guys as well as the bad.

Sure, you'll never get all of the baddies, but what are a few chewed leaves between friends? Think of them as decoration.

OTHER CONTROL METHODS

Biological control is effective but takes a while to kick in. Sometimes you need a speedy response to a pest problem. If the nuisances are big enough to handle (caterpillars and cockroaches, for example), don a pair of gloves, grab a jar or bag to hold the miscreants and deal with them by hand. Depending on your preferences, you might let them go, feed them to the chooks, squash them or kill them in hot, soapy water.

Here are some suggestions for controlling pests without getting your hands messy.

Jar technique

The jar technique is useful in situations where a critter is somewhere it shouldn't be and you don't want to kill it. A wandering spider or beetle in the house, for example. All you need is a clear plastic or glass jar of an appropriate size to contain the unwelcome visitor and a piece of stiff card big enough to cover the jar mouth. The card has to be the right thickness. Neither too thin nor too thick, for reasons that will become apparent in a moment. Christmas or birthday cards are just right.

Carefully lower the jar over the critter until the jar lip is in contact with the surface on which the animal is sitting.

(This technique works best on a smooth, flat surface.) If it's a slow mover, this will be a breeze. It won't be quite so easy if you're dealing with a skittish spider or centipede or a flying insect such as a bee. Take it slowly and steadily. Just as their sudden movements might surprise you, any rapid activity from you is going to scare the living daylights out of them.

Having confined the critter, slide the card between the jar lip and the surface. Do this slowly, so the animal has a chance to get out of the way. Now, this is the tricky bit. You have to turn the jar the right way up without letting the captive escape. And this is why the card has to be the right thickness. If the card's too thin it might buckle when you turn the jar the right way up. If it's too thick, you'll have to lift up the jar to slide it under. That leaves a gap . . . and off it goes!

Barriers and fences

Instead of killing pests, put up barriers and fences to exclude them from selected areas.

Some barriers are cheap and cheerful. Snails and slugs don't like to cross sawdust or wood ash, so a wide, thick band of either of these substances laid around precious seedlings should keep the pests at bay.

Millipedes and slaters have difficulty climbing on

smooth surfaces. (All those feet and no grip!) Wide plastic tape set on its side presents them with an obstacle more challenging to them than Mount Everest. The tape must be at least 50 mm wide. Stand it on something they can't dig through or they might tunnel their way under the fence in a reverse 'Great Escape'. (If you find a tiny vaulting horse, you know you've got trouble on your hands.)

Mosquito nets and wire or fibreglass screens work with most insects, although tiny black flies and sand flies can squeeze through the mesh. Check periodically for rips and loose edges. If there are any weaknesses, something unwanted will invariably find its way through.

Larger nets spread over fruit trees help keep the crop safe from birds, possums and flying foxes. Knitted nets with a mesh size of 40 mm or less are best. White stands out against the leaves, so animals know it is there. Keep the net taut to stop them getting caught in it. It is also important that the net doesn't touch the fruit or they'll be able to nibble or peck through the mesh. Shade cloth—30 per cent block-out—is a cheaper alternative. For more information about netting, check with your state environment or primary industries department.

Fences can be costly and may require a great deal of effort to set up and maintain, but are useful for keeping away larger animals. Information about the best ways to construct a pest-proof fence is available by the truckload in books and on the Web so let's stick to the basics here.

It is important to match the fence to the pest. A plain wire fence may be excellent for confining stock but it is no good for excluding pests. They will crawl through it or jump over it. Pest-proof fences are usually ring-lock wire. The size of the mesh and the height of the fence depend on the type of problem animal. Cat, fox and dog fences are around 2 m high. Rabbit-proof fences can be lower.

Most mammals will burrow under fences, so the wire must either extend at least 45 cm into the soil or another layer of mesh be laid down on top of the soil to prevent digging. For expert climbers and leapers (such as cats), angle the top 50 cm as an overhang. This should stop them scrambling over.

Keeping out kangaroos and wallabies can be a struggle. Not only can they jump over most fences but they will also push them down. Visibility is important in 'roo fencing. If they can't see the wire, they may crash into it, injuring themselves and damaging the fence.

The most effective fences are constructed so that kangaroos can't get in the right spot to jump over them. Sloping fences with the top angled away work well. As do parallel fences, in which the outer one is lower than the inner. In neither design can the kangaroo approach close enough to clear the top.

Whatever their configuration, barriers and fences do need regular maintenance. Things don't always go as planned. Native tree snails in Moorea (French Polynesia) were being preyed on by introduced carnivorous snails, so scientists enclosed an area of forest with a battery-powered electric fence to keep the natives in and the invaders out. Unfortunately, the fence broke when a branch fell across it . . .

Traps

Traps are handy for dealing with infestations in house and garden. Instead of chasing pests around, make them come to you.

The simplest traps are those that provide their target with somewhere to hide. Unsuspecting critters crawl in, expecting to find a comfortable little resting place—which they do—until they discover that all is not quite what it seems. If that sounds like hard work, remember that those traps don't have to be complex. We're not talking about a three-storey Gothic mansion with hidden doors and secret passageways. A trap could be as simple as a plant pot set on its side among the undergrowth or wet newspapers laid down on the lawn. The first type lures snails, whereas the second is good for slaters, earwigs and flatworms. (It's also an excellent weed suppressor and mulch. But I digress.)

Colour plays a part in luring white fly. The little sap-suckers have a thing for yellow and head toward it. Commercially available sticky traps exploit this penchant. You can do the same. Get an empty can, paint the inside bright yellow and smear it with a thin layer of Vaseline. Hang it up near a white-fly-infested plant to keep down pest numbers.

Baited traps are a step up from that. They rely on pests following the scents of something they really want, preferably an item they find utterly irresistible. These might be aromas given off by food or the perfumes of potential mates. This latter method, which uses biological signals called pheromones, has the advantage of targeting individual species rather than attracting a range of them.

Traps work well for cockroaches (p. 76), flies (p. 104) and European wasps (p. 119). The design is a matter of taste (no pun intended) and ingenuity. Pitfall traps, which can be constructed from glass jars, plastic bottles and margarine containers, rely on animals being unable to climb the smooth sides to escape. (Obviously, they don't work with flying insects.) More elaborate traps are completely enclosed, except for a funnel-shaped entrance. Easy to find the way in; not to easy to find the way out.

Baits vary between species. Cockroaches and fruit flies love bananas. Wasps like honey thinned with water. Blowflies go for everything, but a bit of pongy meat is a favourite.

If the category of 'food' is extended to include beer, you can add snails and slugs to the list. Leave out a dish of the amber fluid in the garden overnight and count the haul the next morning. Don't worry about slippery sides or funnel entrances or any of those tricky trap features—the snails drink too much and drown. It's simple. And may not be such a bad end for the slimy pests.

Pheromones are employed in moth traps. Although many insects use these scents in communication, moths are partial to perfumes for sending courtship messages. Male moths pick up the aroma with their antennae and track it back to the source. In this case, the source is a sticky trap. The moths turn up expecting to find a friendly partner and end up glued to a sheet of paper.

These traps are useful for Indian meal moths, whose caterpillars feed on dry food in the pantry, and clothes moths, whose young dine on fabrics (p. 29). Hang them up and set them, but be prepared for swarms—moths can pick up those pheromones from a long way off.

Baits without traps

Baits also work on their own if they are laced with something lethal to pests. Ants (p. 62) are particularly susceptible because they carry baits back to share with their nest mates. Many ready-made baits are available in stores, including those that contain the natural bug-killer *spinosad* (extracted from bacteria). Alternatively, you can mix up your own (not so fancy) bait using a combination of sugar, water and boric acid. Because the sweetness makes it attractive to other species, place the mixture in a sealed container perforated with holes big enough to allow access for ants but too small for other animals. Baits take a while to work—sometimes weeks in the case of large colonies—but are very effective. Boric acid is poisonous so take care when using it. Always wear gloves, and use disposable containers when mixing up and handling baits.

Cockroaches will feed on the same mixture. (Let's face it, they'll feed on anything.) Once again, ensure that the bait is placed where children, pets and non-target animals can't get to it.

Several different types of off-the-shelf snail and slug baits are offered in nurseries and hardware stores. They use different chemicals to control the pests. Those based on iron phosphates are safer for pets and wildlife than those containing metaldehyde and methiocarb. Whichever you chose, make sure they are kept away from the wrong targets. Placing the baits in agricultural pipe or flowerpots laid on their sides reduces that risk.

Scents

Scents are also useful as a way of deterring pests—as long as you (and your immediate neighbours) can cope with the smell.

Ants lay down scent trails when they locate food. These provide guides for their nest mates, so all the others have to do is follow the track to *X* on the map. By interfering with this mechanism, you might be able to create so much confusion among the ants that they give up and move off. Strong aromas such as lavender and eucalyptus oil will overwhelm their signals. And they don't smell too bad.

Stronger pongs have been used to discourage mammals. Success varies not only between species (what deters a kangaroo may not work on a possum) but also between individuals of that species. It all comes down to 'personality'—and hunger. As you can imagine, it's more difficult to deter a starving possum than it is to put off one that's only snacking.

Really stinky stuff is the most effective. Quassia chips, naphthalene and plant fertiliser based on fish or blood and bone are reported to work, although not on all mammals and not all of the time. Be careful if you have dogs, of course. The worst stench in the world is perfume to them! These are smells you don't want to bring inside.

Carnivore poo is supposed to be effective against some animals. Once they get a whiff of a predator around the place they keep away from it. (Understandably.) Chemicals extracted from tiger poo have been tested successfully on feral goats. Whether they work on possums is another matter. So unless you've got a game park or a zoo, you're stuck with the old blood and bone.

Unfortunately, none of these deterrents is a sure-fire solution. You'll have to experiment to work out which (if any) is the most effective against your problem animals.

Scarers

A good scarecrow makes birds think twice before raiding your fruit trees or vegie patch. They're fun to make—stuff some old clothes with straw and prop up your scarecrow where the birds are causing problems. But birds learn quickly that stationary objects—no matter how much they resemble humans—are not a threat. Even the most lifelike of statues soon hosts a party of perching pigeons. So the trick is to give a scarecrow the impression of movement, just to keep the birds on their toes.

Liven up your creation with ribbons to create action. Fluorescent flagging tape is good, as is reflective tape, which shimmers in the sunlight. Just be careful that birds don't get tangled in it, if they decide to fight back.

If you're not keen on a scarecrow (and they *can* look a bit creepy), try stringing the tape from tethered balloons. The balloons will bob around on the breeze. With luck, they'll move enough to startle fruit-stealing birds. For extra 'boo' factor, draw faces on them.

Most birds are frightened by hawks and other birds of prey. Use this natural fear to move them on. You can buy bird scarers in the shapes of owls or hovering hawks, or make something yourself. It can be as elaborate as your skills allow. Place them on television aerials, dangle them from trees or string them over the vegie patch to keep away feathered pests.

Sprays

Sprays are a good way of controlling small, numerous pests, such as scale insects (p. 198) or aphids (p. 74). Unfortunately, they are not specific in their targets, so will usually affect everything. Use them carefully to minimise the impact on the good bugs.

You don't have to spend up big on off-the-shelf products. Some of these are easy to make at home.

Coffee—the good stuff, not leftover grounds—is a handy chemical control for slugs and other soft-bodied animals. Caffeine is produced by coffee bushes to deter seed-eaters, so using as a pest spray is just an extension of its natural function. Mix up one cup of strong coffee to ten cups of water and spray where it's needed.

Garlic spray is made from garlic juice and water. Crush a whole garlic bulb and boil it in a litre of water. When it has cooled, strain out the lumps (or they'll block the sprayer) and dilute it in four litres of water. You can substitute chillies. Or combine the two for a super strong pest spray.

White oil is a mix of vegetable oil and soap. Combine a cup of vegetable oil and half a cup of water with a teaspoon (5 ml) of dishwashing detergent to make a concentrate. Then use the mixture in a dilution of one tablespoon (20 ml) to a litre of warm water. Soap acts as a surfactant. Not only does it help to keep the oil in suspension but also it breaks down the waxy, waterproof coating that covers insects.

Other plant extracts are useful for pest control. Pyrethrins are probably the best known. They are obtained from the seeds of the European chrysanthemum (*Pyrethrum cinerariaefolium*). They are very effective, killing insects on contact by disrupting their nervous systems. Unfortunately, they are not very specific and will eradicate both the goodies and the baddies. They are also poisonous to aquatic animals, so they will harm tadpoles and fish (as well as insects) if they get into ponds and creeks. Pyrethrins are commercially available in two versions: pure and with PBO (*pipronyl butoxide*), which increases their effectiveness.

FIRST AID FOR YOU

Despite Australia's reputation as a country crawling with dangerous wildlife—and let's face it, we love to scare visitors with those stories—most encounters between people and animals are entirely trouble-free. (For the people, at least. Animals don't always fare so well.) Certainly, a few house and garden species are capable of doing damage to us. But even with the most notorious creatures, such as tiger snakes and funnel-web spiders, the majority of meetings result in nothing more than a big shock—for both parties. Only a small percentage of encounters end in injury. And, of those, a tiny number are severe. So far, the odds are in your favour.

Animals don't go out of their way to hurt you. Why would they? You're bigger and heavier than most of them. (Don't be offended. Even toddlers are in a different weight class to critters.) They would rather flee than tangle with a human. Bad experiences are almost always the result of sticking your hand or foot in the wrong place, cornering an animal or giving it a fright.

You can reduce the chances of something going wrong, but accidents do happen. Knowing what to do in these circumstances could mean the difference between life and death.

If you're bitten or stung: don't panic. If someone else is bitten or stung: don't panic. Running around like a headless chook won't help. In fact, it's likely to make the situation worse.

Identify the problem—what sort of animal caused the injury?

Apply first aid appropriate for the injury.

Call for medical assistance if required.

. . . And don't panic.

ANTS, BEES AND WASPS

The effect of the sting is disproportionate to the size of the stinger!

Ants will hold on with their jaws (ouch!) while they jab in the poison. Like wasps, they have smooth, needle-like stings that can be used multiple times. A bee's sting ends in a backward pointing barb that anchors it so it can't be withdrawn from the skin. When a bee tries to leave—or is assisted in leaving—the sting remains in place together with the poison sac. The sac continues to contract, pumping in venom with every squeeze. Remove the sting and venom apparatus by sliding your fingernail under it and flicking it out. Pinching it between thumb and forefinger will result in more poison being injected.

Wash the site with soap and water. A cold pack will reduce pain and swelling at the site of the sting. Do not put ice directly onto the skin because that will cause more damage.

Antihistamines, available over the counter from pharmacies, will ease persistent local symptoms. Get advice from the pharmacist about the best type. Analgesics (aspirin, paracetamol et cetera) may also help with the pain.

Get medical help immediately if the victim has previously experienced a severe reaction to stings, has been stung several times or has been stung in the mouth or throat. (This might happen if an insect enters a can of soft drink.)

Even if there is no history of problems, watch for symptoms of an allergic reaction. These include an itchy rash that spreads beyond the immediate site of the sting, swollen lips and eyelids, dizziness and shortness of breath. If these occur, medical attention is required.

CATERPILLARS

They don't bite or sting, but many species of caterpillars are covered with hairs and spines that cause itching and inflammation on contact.

If hairs are embedded in the skin, pick out the larger ones with tweezers. If that doesn't work—or if there are too many—try removing them with adhesive tape. Don't scratch the affected area, no matter how much it itches, because you may end up pushing stray hairs further into your skin. You also increase the chance of infection. Once you've cleared out the hairs, wash the affected area with soap and water. Antihistamines may counteract much of the irritation.

Do not touch your eyes if you have encountered stinging caterpillars. If hairs drift into the eye, get medical help immediately.

As always, keep a close watch for allergic reactions.

CENTIPEDES AND SCORPIONS

Their bites (centipedes) and stings (scorpions) are painful but aren't usually serious.

Wash the wound with soap and water, and apply a cold pack to reduce pain and swelling. Bacterial infections may be a problem—remember where those stings and claws have been! Visit your general practitioner if the inflammation spreads. Always make sure your tetanus vaccinations are up to date.

Keep watch for allergic reactions (see Ants, bees and wasps, p. 221), which may require urgent medical intervention.

LEECHES

Leech bites continue to bleed long after the little sucker has had its fill and dropped off. The wounds look horrible, and sometimes you think they will *never* stop bleeding. But they do . . . eventually.

As with all other injuries that damage the skin, they are vulnerable to infection. Wash the bite with soap and water to reduce the chances of this happening. Local pressure will slow blood flow, if that's a problem.

Watch for allergic reactions (see Ants, bees and wasps, p. 221).

SNAKES

Don't panic. I've said it before but it's worth repeating.

Remember: not all snakes are poisonous. Not every bite from a poisonous snake results in injection of a dangerous amount of venom. The snake's teeth might not break the skin, or the bite might be 'dry'. (Venom is an important resource. They don't just throw it around.)

Anti-venoms are available for all dangerous snakes in Australia.

Treat a bite as if it were from a venomous snake. That minimises the risk from a wrong identification.

Wrap a bandage around the affected area to slow down the spread of venom. You can apply the bandage over clothing. Don't wrap it too tightly or you'll cut off the blood supply, which may cause more problems than the bite itself. The idea is to slow down the spread of venom through the body.

Immobilise an affected limb with a splint (for a leg or arm) or sling (for an arm). Call for medical assistance. Do not remove the bandage. The doctor will do this when appropriate treatment is at hand.

DO NOT wash the wound. The hospital will identify the type of anti-venom required from the dried venom left on the victim's skin.

DO NOT cut the wound to drain or suck out the poison. This increases the risk of infection.

DO NOT drink alcohol.

DO NOT try to catch the snake. That's an excellent way to get bitten.

SPIDERS

Although spider bites are painful, few of them are dangerous. For most bites, treatment need be no more complex than washing the wound with soap and water, applying a cold pack and watching for signs of an allergic reaction (see Ants, bees and wasps, p. 221).

Redback and funnel-web spider bites are more serious. Anti-venom is available for both species.

Not all redback spider bites require immediate treatment. Often the symptoms are no worse than localised pain and swelling (although that's bad enough). Treat these as indicated above, and keep an eye open for any negative change.

Immediate medical treatment is necessary if the victim develops any of the following symptoms: swollen or tender glands in armpit or groin; intense pain spreading out from the bite; sweating, shivering or shaking; nausea; pins and needles in limbs; or severe headache. Attention is also important if the victim has an underlying medical condition (such as kidney, heart or blood pressure problems) or is pregnant, even if they show none of these symptoms. As they say, better safe than sorry.

All funnel-web spider bites should be regarded as dangerous, even though the impact of the venom depends on the age and sex of the spider. (How good are you at judging those in emergency circumstances?) As with snake bite, use the pressure–immobilisation technique of firmly wrapping the affected area with a bandage and keeping it motionless with a splint or sling. The bandage should not come off until anti-venom or other treatment is available.

Don't panic. Remember: no one has died from a funnel-web bite since anti-venom was developed in 1981.

TICKS

After removing ticks, watch for allergic reactions. If the victim is sluggish, has difficulty in walking or swallowing or has blurred vision, seek medical assistance. Anti-venom is available for the paralysis tick.

FIRST AID FOR (NON-SPINELESS) ANIMALS

Injured or distressed wildlife occasionally turn up around the house and garden. Always have handy the telephone number of the local vet or wildlife rescue service. Put it on speed dial in your mobile phone.

You may have to catch the injured animal and take it to the vet or carer. Try to minimise the suffering of the already distressed creature. (Yours too. It's not much fun dealing with an injured animal.) On catching it, place it in a well-ventilated, secure box or cage with suitable bedding. Say goodbye to any towels or pillowcases used in the process. They will never be the same again.

Keep the animal warm and in the dark. When transporting it, make sure that there are no bumps, sudden noises or changes in temperature.

COLLISIONS WITH WINDOWS

Birds sometimes fly into windows at full pelt. Although often fatal, sometimes the bird is only stunned by the impact. If so, place it somewhere quiet and safe from predators (not only cats and dogs but also crows, magpies and other birds). Make sure it's also away from ant nests. It will soon recover and fly away.

In some cases, the bird takes several hours or more to recuperate. Put the bird in a box in a darkened room, where it won't be disturbed. Check on its progress after a few hours. A badly injured bird requires veterinary treatment.

You can reduce the chances of birds colliding with windows by fitting insect screens or external blinds.

ENCOUNTERS WITH CATS AND DOGS

Possums and birds often come off badly in encounters with dogs and cats. Treat grazes and other shallow wounds with warm salt water. (The patient won't thank you, but this treatment reduces the chances of infection.) Because of the risk of infection, especially from bites, take the injured animal to a vet.

FALLEN CHICKS

A chick is sitting on the ground. It's making plaintive *peep-peep* calls. Clearly too young to fend for itself, it's a target for any passing cat or dog. You can't see its parents anywhere. What do you do?

Often one or both parents will be nearby. Place the chick in a shallow box and secure the container in a tree. Worried that the parents might reject a chick that smells of humans? Most birds have a very ordinary sense of smell. They probably won't even notice.

ORPHANS AND WAIFS

Rearing abandoned or orphaned mammals and birds is hard work. Yes, it's rewarding, but it can also be heartbreaking. Be realistic about your abilities. Are you dedicated enough? Do you have the right (emotional) stuff? Do you understand the effort required? If the answer to any of those questions starts with . . . um . . . then this is not the right time to become a wildlife carer.

In most states, you will need a licence to look after protected animals, even if your intention is to release them when they are old enough to take care of themselves. (There are links to the relevant government agencies on p. 236.) In the ACT, for example, to become a registered carer, you must be trained first by the RSPCA.

Until you're ready to take on the commitment, it is in everyone's best interest to deliver the foundling to a carer or vet.

FIND OUT MORE

General

Harvey, MS and Yen, AL (1989) *Worms to Wasps: An illustrated guide to Australia's terrestrial invertebrates*, Oxford University Press.

Horne, PA and Crawford, DJ (2005) *Backyard Insects*, Miegunyah Press.

Museums Victoria (2006) *Melbourne's Wildlife: A fieldguide to the fauna of greater Melbourne,* Museums Victoria and CSIRO.

Queensland Museum (1995) *Wildlife of Greater Brisbane*, Queensland Museum.

Queensland Museum (2000) *Wildlife of Tropical North Queensland: Cooktown to Mackay*, Queensland Museum.

Temby, I (2005) *Wild Neighbours: The humane approach to living with wildlife*, Citrus Press.

Wildlife of Sydney, <http//faunanet.gov.au/wos/index.cfm> Australian Museum Online, date accessed 9 March 2009.

Zborowski, P (2002) *Insects of Australia*, Green Guide series, New Holland.

Zborowski, P and Storey, R (2003) *A Field Guide to Insects in Australia*, New Holland.

Long and thin

Millipedes of Australia, <www.qvmag.tas.gov.au/zoology/millipedes/index.html>, date accessed 9 March 2009.

Tasmanian multipedes, <www.qvmag.tas.gov.au/zoology/multipedes/mulintro.html>, date accessed 9 March 2009.

Hoppers, skippers and jumpers

Rentz, DCF (1996) *Grasshopper Country: The abundant orthopteroid insects of Australia*, UNSW Press.

Eight-legged crawlers

Brunet, B (2000) *Spiderwatch: A guide to Australian Spiders*, New Holland.

Lindsey, T (2001) *Spiders of Australia*, Green Guide series, New Holland.

Walker, KL, Yen, AL and Milledge, GA (2003) *Spiders and Scorpions Commonly Found in Victoria*, Royal Society of Victoria.

Six-legged crawlers

Australian Ants Online: The guide to the Australian ant fauna, <www.ento.csiro.au/science/ants/default.htm>, CSIRO, date accessed 9 March 2009.

Coleoptera: Beetles and weevils, <www.ento.csiro.au/

education/insects/coleoptera_families/coleoptera_families.html>, CSIRO, date accessed 9 March 2009.

Slipinski, A, Hastings, A and Boyd, B, *Ladybirds of Australia*, <www.ento.csiro.au/biology/ladybirds/lady birds.htm>, CSIRO, date accessed 9 March 2009.

Braby, MF (2004) *The Complete Guide to Butterflies of Australia*, CSIRO.

Greenslade, PJM (1998) *A Guide to Ants of South Australia*, South Australian Museum.

Hawkeswood, T (1987) *Beetles of Australia*, Angus & Robertson.

Moulds, MS (1990) *Australian Cicadas*, UNSW Press.

Zborowski, P and Edwards, T (2007) *A Guide to Australian Moths*, CSIRO.

Snails and slugs

Smith, BJ and Kershaw, RC (1979) *Field Guide to the Non-marine Molluscs of South-eastern Australia*, Australian National University Press.

Fliers

Australian Moths Online <www.ento.csiro.au/anic/moths.html>, CSIRO, date accessed 9 March 2009.

Australian Native Bee Research Centre, <www.aussiebee.com.au>, date accessed 9 March 2009.

Australian Native Bees, <www.australiannativebees.com/N_main.php>, date accessed 9 March 2009.

Victorian Butterflies, <http://museumvictoria.com.au/bioinformatics/butter>, date accessed 9 March 2009.

Common, IFB (1990) *Moths of Australia*, Melbourne University Press.

Daley, E (2007) *Wings: An introduction to Tasmania's winged insects*, Riffles.

Herbison-Evans, D and Crossley, S, *Butterfly Larvae of Australia*, <www-staff.it.uts.edu.au/~don/larvae/butter.html>, date accessed 9 March 2009.

Herbison-Evans, D and Crossley, S, *Caterpillars of Australian Moths*, <www-staff.it.uts.edu.au/~don/larvae/moths.html>, date accessed 9 March 2009.

Theischinger, G and Hawking, J (2006) *The Complete Field Guide to Dragonflies of Australia*, CSIRO.

Not the Spineless

Anstis, M (2002) *Tadpoles of South-eastern Australia: A guide with keys,* New Holland.

Barker, JSF, Grigg, G and Tyler, M (1995) *A Field Guide to Australian Frogs*, Surrey Beatty & Sons.

Canberra Birds Photo Gallery <http://photogallery.canberrabirds.org.au>, Canberra Ornithologists Group, date accessed 9 March 2009.

Egerton, L (2004) *Know Your Birds: Australia's Most Common Birds*, New Holland.

Frogs Australia Network, Frog Field Guides, <www.frogsaustralia.net.au/frogs/field-guides.cfm>, date accessed 9 March 2009.

Frogs of Victoria, <http://museumvictoria.com.au/bioinformatics/rfvic>, date accessed 9 March 2009.

Australian Lizards—The Victorian fauna of Lizards, Geckos, Skinks, Dragons, Goannas, Monitors and Legless Lizards, <http://museumvictoria.com.au/bioinformatics/lizards>, date accessed 9 March 2009.

Australian Mammals—The Victorian fauna, <http://museumvictoria.com.au/bioinformatics/mammals/index.htm>, date accessed 9 March 2009.

Australian Snakes—The Victorian fauna, <http://museumvictoria.com.au/bioinformatics/snake>, date accessed 9 March 2009.

Swan, G (2001) *Frogs of Australia*, Green Guide series, New Holland.

Swan, G (1998) *Snakes and Other Reptiles of Australia*, Green Guide series, New Holland.

Walraven, E (1999) *Care of Australian Wildlife*, New Holland.

State government organisations

Australian Capital Territory

Department of Territory and Municipal Services <www.tams.act.gov.au>

RSPCA ACT <www.rspca-act.org.au>

New South Wales

Department of Environment and Climate Change <www.environment.nsw.gov.au>

NSW Department of Primary Industries <www.dpi.nsw.gov.au>

Northern Territory

Natural Resources, Environment, the Arts and Sport <www.nt.gov.au/nreta/parks/index.html>

Regional Development, Primary Industry, Fisheries and Resources <www.nt.gov.au/d>

Queensland

Department of Primary Industries and Fisheries <www.dpi.qld.gov.au>

Environmental Protection Agency <www.epa.qld.gov.au>

South Australia

Department for Environment and Heritage <www.environment.sa.gov.au>

Department of Primary Industries and Resources SA <www.pir.sa.gov.au>

Tasmania

Department of Primary Industries and Water <www.dpiw.tas.gov.au>

Victoria

Department of Primary Industries <www.dpi.vic.gov.au/dpi>

Department of Sustainability and Environment <www.dse.vic.gov.au>

Western Australia

Department of Agriculture and Food <www.agric.wa.gov.au>

Department of Environment and Conservation <www.dec.wa.gov.au>

Museum sites

State museums are excellent sources of information about the Spineless. Most have information centres where you can take things for identification. Some also have fact sheets available online.

Australian Museum, College Street, Sydney, NSW <www.amonline.net.au>

Museum Victoria: Melbourne Museum, Nicholson Street, Carlton, Vic <http://museumvictoria.com.au>

South Australian Museum, North Terrace, Adelaide, SA <www.samuseum.sa.gov.au>

Western Australian Museum, Perth Cultural Centre, James Street, Perth, WA <www.museum.wa.gov.au>

Museums and Art Galleries of the Northern Territory, Darwin, NT <www.nt.gov.au/nreta/museums>

Queensland Museum, South Bank, Brisbane, Qld <www.southbank.qm.qld.gov.au>

Museum of Tropical Queensland, Flinders Street, Townsville, Qld <www.mtq.qm.qld.gov.au>

Queen Victoria Museum and Art Gallery, Launceston, Tas <www.qvmag.tas.gov.au>

Tasmanian Museum and Art Gallery, Macquarie Street, Hobart, Tas <www.tmag.tas.gov.au>

INDEX

Printed in Dunstable, United Kingdom

89705172R00145